Disney
Bound

Dress Disney and Make It Fashion

Disney Bound

Dress Disney and Make It Fashion

Leslie Kay

EDITIONS

LOS ANGELES • NEW YORK

This book is dedicated to the Disney-bounding community.
Disney-bounding is what it is today thanks to your creativity.
You are true Disney magic makers!

This book is also dedicated to Jim Weiss and John Vignocchi
for being the best mentors ever. It wouldn't
have been possible without both of you!

Contents

VIII
Foreword

XI
Introduction

1
1 Disney-Bounding Steps

23
2 The Importance of Accessories

49
3 Personal Style

63
4 Tips and Tricks

71

5 Bounding Around the World

109

6 Taking Your Bound to the Next Level

133

7 The Community

151

8 The Disney-Bounding Inauguration

154
Acknowledgments

155
Bounders

156
Index

Foreword

I simply didn't know what "Disney-bounding" was.

In spite of my reputation as a "Disney Authority," at a certain time not so long ago, my age, along with personal and professional preoccupations, put me in a place where this phenomenon was a mystery to me.

I heard it being referred to, discussed, and debated but I never dug deeper. Like "Dapper Days," I had a vague sense that it was some sort of event-based variation of "dressing up to go to the Park," or that it was a Disney-specific offshoot of cosplay—in any case, Disney-bounding was not part of my culture or experience.

Then one day, fate stepped in, as she often does, and my friends at The Walt Disney Studios asked me to host a group of young "influencers" at Disneyland—and I met a troupe of passionate, talented, creative people who not only showed me what Disney-bounding is, but enlightened me about the whole craft and culture surrounding this phenomenon.

A wonderful personality named Leslie Kay was the bright light at the center of this group—and I learned a lot that afternoon.

Disney-bounding, in its simplest definition, is making a "street-wearable" fashion that reflects and portrays a Disney character or experience.

In my book *The Art of Disney Costuming: Heroes, Villains, and Spaces Between*, I wrote, "In all the varied narrative media of Disney, costumes are as significant and memorable an element of building a character and telling a story as any other aspect, from script to sound and from performance to production design."

Although Disney-bounding is similar to building a character and telling a story, it's not "costume"—in many ways, it is more complicated than cosplay, because it relies on the complete concept realization, design, and fabrication of the apparel elements that constitute a finished, polished, and subtly recognizable "look."

Disney-bounding is a similar craft to costuming, but it's a translation to another storytelling medium. It relies not on the making of a literal replica of a well-known wardrobe, but in the creation of nuanced visual cues in color, shape, texture, and materials; and the relationships of these things to one another, in order to evoke a visual reminder or stimulate an emotional memory—even before any literal character connection is seen.

And that's not easy.

Oscar-winning songwriter and Disney Legend Robert B. Sherman once said to me, "It takes a lot of work to write a 'simple' song."

Disney-bounding is like that. At its most successful, the craft of it seems almost invisible, effortless—but it is an effort. The design is highly informed, thoughtful, clever, and erudite; research, study, and plain hard work go into the making of a successful Bound.

In the same way, Leslie Kay's book is as sprightly, charming, and passionate as the author and the subject, but beneath that is a wealth of information about the origins, and much of her fundamental philosophy of Disney-bounding; it also gives an expert's advice about how to design and craft these remarkable creations yourself.

For generations, Disney stories, characters, and experiences have inspired audiences around the world with curiosity, imagination, and creativity.

This enchanting volume (and by extension, Disney-bounding as an art form) frees one to celebrate and honor favorite Disney characters and memories—along with granting an inspiring and liberating permission to fearlessly explore, to vigorously imagine, and to passionately create.

What could be more *Disney* than that?

Jeff Kurtti
Disney Legacy Authority
Author of The Art of Disney Costuming: Heroes, Villains, and Spaces Between

Introduction

For those new to Disney-bounding, I want to take a moment to introduce myself. I'm Leslie Kay, the face behind the *DisneyBound* blog!

I'm a Disney fan, just like you are. When I was a child, you could usually find me on a Saturday afternoon locked away in my bedroom playing my *Classic Disney: Volume IV* cassette tape. This was before we had endless song options at our fingertips, so to have an eclectic mix of Disney music on cassette was very special to me. I loved to dance, and to pass the time as a child, I would choreograph performances to that cassette tape . . . and not just one dance for the song—all the characters would have their own roles! The Broadway production didn't stop at choreography. Once I had the choreography down for a song, I would sit down and sketch out the costumes each character would wear in that performance. My love for everything Disney started when I was young, and it has never left me.

I had the opportunity to go to Walt Disney World for the first time when I was ten years old, and I fell in love with it immediately—although you wouldn't have known it based off the first photo ever taken of me on Main Street, U.S.A. As much as I wanted to feel the magic of Walt Disney World again, I wouldn't get to return until I was an adult. At age twenty-two, I had the realization that with my full-time job (and very little actual responsibility at that point), I could use my own money to go to Walt Disney World . . . so I did!

My friend Lizz and I began planning our trip and booked a room at Disney's Port Orleans Resort— Riverside, a resort that I still love very much to this day.

At the time, my day job didn't allow me the opportunity to fully express my creativity. So I started blogging when I got home as a way to creatively channel my excitement for my upcoming trip to Walt Disney World. I turned to the website Tumblr, which had a well-established group of Disney fans, and the blog *DisneyBound* was created. This name came from being literally bound for Disney. However, years later, a fan asked me, "Is your blog name *DisneyBound* for Walt Disney and Lillian Bounds, Lillian Disney's maiden name?" My jaw dropped. I'd had no idea that was her maiden name. The fact that the name accidentally but perfectly pays homage to their love story is one of my favorite little anecdotes about the blog.

The truth is, the Disney-bound concept all started with one outfit. At first, the content that lived on *DisneyBound* was just like any other Disney blog. It featured a lot of fan art, Disney photography, film stills, and other posts along those lines. But one Saturday afternoon, I found myself bursting with excitement for my Disney trip and I had a creative urge. I visited of my favorite fashion websites, Polyvore, with the thought, "What would Rapunzel (the newest princess at the time) wear if she were a girl just like me? What would she wear to the mall? Or out with her friends?" I found images of different clothes, shoes, and accessories online, came up with an outfit, and posted it on my blog. People immediately responded to it. Suddenly, requests came pouring in for *more* princesses . . . and then *more* characters. So I created and posted more looks, and the *DisneyBound* blog quickly grew from a couple hundred followers to a couple thousand. Soon it had tens of thousands of followers, and I found myself going viral. I was on national television three weeks after that initial Rapunzel outfit, talking about the Disney-bounding movement, when I really had no idea what it was or would eventually become beyond just a fun little thought on a Saturday afternoon.

DisneyBound, the blog, has been around for nine years as I sit here and write these words. It's such an incredible way to celebrate a wild and crazy Disney journey. It's important for me to mention that the spirit behind Disney-bounding belongs to everyone; the *DisneyBound* blog simply allowed the concept to live and grow. It went from a little touch of Disney magic in everyone's wardrobe to a community and a beacon for those with the same interests—a place we could all gather and show off our love for Disney.

I was a creative kid who was raised on Winnie the Pooh and Disney Sing-Along Songs, so it's probably not shocking to many around me that I have based my career on being a huge fan of Disney. But you might be surprised to know I spent much of my childhood unsure if I would ever amount to anything at all. Self-confidence was a major issue, and I suffered a lot at the hands of bullies in middle school. It's because of this that I wanted to make sure I was using this platform for a good reason. I will always try my best to spread the word of positivity and self-care through Disney-bounding—you'll see this throughout the book.

The song "Go the Distance" from *Hercules* was on that favorite cassette tape of mine, and it still brings me to tears, but for different reasons than it did when I was eight years old. Now when I hear it, I remember being that young girl dancing to that song in her bedroom, hoping someday she could go the distance and someday find the place where she belonged. It would be many years later that I actually found my place through the magic of Disney and among the best and most creative people I've ever met.

This book is my way of sharing my love of Disney and Disney-bounding with the Bounding community and Bounders-to-be, with how-tos, tips, and loads of inspiration. I hope it helps you put together your best Bounds ever, and have as much fun as possible in the space where fashion and Disney collide.

Important Park Lingo

I'll be using terms throughout this book that you can't find in any ordinary dictionary, so here is the Disney-bounder's dictionary to help break it down for you.

Disney-bound (n)

A Disney-bound (also referred to as a "Bound") is an outfit—but *not* a full costume—inspired by your favorite Disney character using items that you can find in your own closet or at your local mall.

Disney-bounding or Bounding (v)

The action of wearing your Disney-bound or Bound.

Disney-bounder or Bounder (n)

Someone who loves to Disney-bound (example: you, when you finish this book).

Cast Member (n)

A cast member is the Disney version of what you might normally refer to as a "staff member." Disney is so much more than a place of work, though. Every cast member is part of the big picture—the show!—and is integral to making sure the show runs smoothly.

Backstage (n)

When you're visiting a Disney Park, any place where guests are not permitted to go is referred to as "backstage." Most guests will never be taken backstage, but if you do have the opportunity, it's important to note that cameras or video gear are not permitted back there.

Guest (n)

If you are not a cast member, then you are a guest while visiting a Disney Park. You are more than a person attending a theme park—you are a guest on their property, and the cast members will try to make your day as magical as they possibly can!

Magical Express (n)

If you're visiting Walt Disney World, make sure to call ahead and book your spot on the Magical Express. This is a shuttle that makes getting to and from Orlando International Airport seamless!

Extra Magic Hours (n)

If you are staying at a Disney Resort hotel, you'll want to ask about Extra Magic Hours, available only to Disney hotel guests. They will be either in the morning (before the park opens) or the evening (after it closes). It's a great way to add a little more Disney Parks fun to your day, without large crowds.

DVC (Disney Vacation Club) (n)

When visiting the Disney Parks, you might hear some guests refer to DVC—Disney Vacation Club. Anyone can join! Keep your eyes peeled for the information booths about this amazing prepaid Disney vacation plan.

FastPass+™ (n)

A FastPass+ works as a line bypass ticket. It allows you to skip the main line and stand in a much shorter line if you arrive during your assigned time. They book up fast, so make sure to reserve them as soon as you can. You can book your FastPass+™ selections sixty days in advance, if you are staying at a Disney property.

MagicBand (n)

If you stay at a Disney Resort hotel (or you're an Annual Passholder) when visiting Walt Disney World, you will be given a MagicBand. It works as your hotel key, and you can attach a credit card to it if you'd like to charge to your room while you're in the parks.

If you purchase Memory Maker, the photographers will also scan your MagicBand to make sure your photos get to the right spot. MagicBands come in eight colors, and you can visit www.shopdisney.com or the shops at Walt Disney World for an even larger selection of premium options. You can even choose one to match your Disney-bound!

Memory Maker (n)

Memory Maker is a service that provides unlimited digital PhotoPass pictures. It's a great way to get incredible photos of your Disney-bound as you venture through the Disney Parks. It connects to your online Disney account and keeps all your photos in one convenient place.

Hidden Mickeys (n)

Did you know that Disney loves to hide Mickey Mouses EVERYWHERE? Next time you're on a Disney property, keep an eye out for them. They are in the carpets, the drapes, the attractions, the shops, and the scenery.

Rope Drop (n)

This term for the park's opening refers to the idea that there's a rope stretched across the entrance that drops to let you in. You might hear your fellow guests talk about wanting to "make rope drop." Set your alarms if you're hoping to join them! It's a fun experience! (There may not be actual ropes, though.)

Chapter
1

Disney-
Bounding
Steps

So, you want to put together a Disney-bound?

It can be overwhelming at first. Where do you even start with putting together an outfit? Does character accuracy matter? Do you have to look like the character you want to portray? Do you need props? There are SO many character options, and your closet is full of clothes, but where do you even begin? Like anything in the fashion industry, it all starts with a handful of simple steps. When Disney-bounding, you'll use wardrobe staples every Disney style guru should have in their closet to create the looks for your favorite Disney characters. I encourage you to use my words as a guide, but not a rule book. Feel free to make each suggestion your own, or to completely ignore it if it doesn't ring true for who you are and what you like to wear. It's important that you feel like yourself when you're Disney-bounding. It's when you feel like yourself that you'll truly find your confidence.

Disney-bounding is different from cosplay. It's not about being in costume or portraying a character as accurately as possible. If you're unfamiliar with cosplay, it's short for "costume play"—what you'll see folks doing at fandom conventions. Cosplayers are a creative and talented bunch. They usually spend weeks, months, or even years perfecting their costumes so they can show them off to the world while bringing the characters to life. The world is so much

more fun because cosplayers are in it! With Disney-bounding, though, you're not aiming for character accuracy, and character wigs and props are not needed. (In fact, most of the time costumes aren't even allowed for Disney Park guests who are fourteen or older.) Just have fun with your personal style and the items that are easily accessible to you. It's a casual way to take on a Disney character's favorite fashions while going about your daily life. Maybe people will recognize you're dressed as a Disney character . . . maybe they won't. Disney-bounding is not about being recognized, but about how your outfit makes you feel on the inside. You don't need to create the clothing items from scratch or even purchase them at all. A lot of the time, you'll have a Disney character in your closet just waiting to be discovered!

A good rule of thumb for putting together your Disney-bound is keeping comfort in mind. What would you feel comfortable wearing to the mall or out and about with friends? If you feel comfortable wearing that clothing in those situations, then you've found the Disney-bound style that works for you!

Disney-bounding can be done ANYWHERE in the world. While many of those who Disney-bound love to do it when they visit the Disney Parks, you can explore your love for your favorite Disney character through fashion wherever you may be! Disney-bounders have worn their Bounds to the movies, the mall, prom, weddings, graduations, vacations, cruises . . . the list goes on and on. If it's a special occasion and you feel the draw to add a little extra Disney magic to your day, Bound away! There are also Disney-bounders all over the world—from California to Tokyo, England to Australia. Wherever you find yourself in the world, odds are there's a Disney-bounder near you ready for some Disney fashion fun!

At its most basic, Disney-bounding uses color blocking, accessories, and your own added touch to show your love of Disney in a unique way. Of course I'll give you tons of tips and tricks, but at the end of the day it's your personal style that matters the most.

Step One
Choosing a Character OR a Key Item

Where you begin with your Disney-bound is up to you! Some Bounders like to start by picking the character they'd like to Bound. This might be a character they idolize, or maybe a character they feel represents them. Other Bounders might select a character based on the park they'll be visiting or activity they plan to do.

Other times, Disney-bounding will start with a key item of clothing that you know will be the perfect piece for a specific character. Now that you're a Disney-bounder, you'll never look at clothing the same way again! As you walk through the mall or you look through your own closet, you'll start to see many characters jumping out at you. So perhaps your Disney-bounding adventure will begin with a character choosing you—instead of you choosing a character.

Step Two
Color Blocking

Color blocking is the art of using a combination of colors, often very different from each other, to design a unique and interesting outfit. With Disney-bounding, we take that a step further. We use color blocking to create the stylized foundation of the way a Disney character has been designed. For instance, if you were going to create a Disney-bound for Cruella De Vil, the Disney fashionista herself, you could wear an outfit that is primarily black with a white jacket, red shoes, and a faux-fur accent or something with a Dalmatian print. For the Genie, put a lighter blue on top with a darker blue on bottom, pair it with a red belt and some magical accessories, and ta-da—you're Aladdin's fantastic sidekick! It's all about looking at where colors fall on the character and using that as your guide for creating your Disney fashion masterpiece!

Step Three
Silhouettes

A silhouette describes the shape and construction of a clothing item itself. Sometimes you can re-create silhouettes that you see on your favorite Disney characters. Take a look at the Disney character you're looking to Disney-bound. Explore the unique shapes and details their outfits possess. Using Aurora, for example—her gown offers a beautiful off-the-shoulder silhouette, which might translate over to a dress with a similar structure. Snow White, on the other hand, has voluminous short sleeves on her gown. Perhaps you can find a blue shirt with a little volume in the sleeves to pay homage to that detail when building your Snow White Disney-bound. Using silhouettes is a great way to give your Disney-bound an extra dimension, but it's not always a must-do.

Step Four
Accessories

Beyond color blocking and silhouettes, there is a lot of detail that can come from the accessories you choose. Since you won't be carrying props around, your accessories will become your character's props of choice—be it a weapon, an animal sidekick, or something that your character comes into contact with at one point. Accessories like jewelry, bags, and even socks can tell the same story props would.

Step Five
Overall Vibe

When putting together your Disney-bound, take the overall vibe of your outfit into consideration. Incorporating your own personality and personal style is important, but also take into consideration the personality and style of the character you are trying to embody. If Buzz Lightyear were putting together a Disney-bound, he might opt for more modern pieces, while Robin Hood might be more of a boho-chic Bounder!

Key Pieces

Let's start with the basics: those key pieces that are useful for a variety of Disney-bounds. Who better to discuss the basics of Disney-bounding with than with our original crew of Disney characters: Mickey Mouse, Minnie Mouse, Donald Duck, Daisy Duck and Goofy! I like that these characters can be so easily Bounded without much in the way of accessories. You can never go wrong with the Fab 5!

YELLOW SHOES

Did you ever think that you'd read a style tutorial that would not only list "yellow shoes" as a basic . . . but in fact, list it first, above any other basics? Well, welcome to the wonderful world of Disney-bounding! It wasn't until I started to explore all that goes into the look and style of Disney's catalog of characters that I realized—WOW! There are a lot of yellow Disney characters, or characters who wear yellow! Have you ever thought about how many Disney characters wear yellow shoes or have yellow feet? Just off the top of my head, I can think of a handful! Mickey Mouse, Minnie Mouse, Donald Duck, Belle, Snow White, and Simba are just a few of the many Disney characters who love to show off that sunny shade on their feet. I like to keep a pair of yellow sneakers in my Disney-bounding wardrobe at all times. They're not only cute and stylish but also easy to wear for a day at the Disney Parks.

Of course, everyone has a different level of comfort. You don't have to purchase the first pair of yellow shoes that feels decent; actually, you don't have to purchase them at all. If yellow shoes are not in your budget, no problem! There are a lot of ways that you can craft your own. (We'll touch on that a little bit later in the book.) Also, don't feel like you MUST wear yellow shoes just because your character does. Mickey Mouse is still Mickey Mouse, even with black sneakers instead of yellow. If you feel like you're giving off a real Mickey vibe, that's all that matters.

BROWN BOOTS

Another shoe style that you'll probably get a lot of wear out of as a Bounder is a pair of brown boots. From Woody to Merida, Goofy to Chewbacca . . . there are so many characters in the Disney rolodex who need a pair of brown ankle boots to complete their Disney-bounded look. This wardrobe item is great because you'll probably get plenty of use out of it in your day-to-day life. Not only is a pair of great brown boots a Disney-bounding staple, it's also a regular fashion staple.

to you and screams "I would be perfect for a Jasmine Disney-bound!" it might be worth the purchase. There is a DIY trick to colored denim, too, which we'll touch on a little bit later. (Hold on to your light-colored or white denim. You never know when you might need them!)

COLORED PANTS

Since Disney-bounding uses a lot of color blocking, colored basics are an obvious must-have for every Disney-bounder. Tees, sweaters, shorts, and hats in unique or hard-to-find colors are a great thing to keep handy. You never know when they could help you transform into your favorite Disney character! I like to stock up on colored denim, especially when I see it on sale in my favorite shops. By having an array of colored denim in your wardrobe, you'll be ready to Disney-bound just about any Disney character at the drop of a hat. Don't worry too much about making sure you have denim in every shade of the rainbow; closet space is precious, so don't take up every inch with denim you hope to use for a Disney character someday. On the other hand, if you see a pair of colored jeans on sale that really speaks

SOLID-COLORED TEES

Similar to colored pants, it's great to have a variety of solid-colored tees in your closet so that you can easily Disney-bound multiple Disney characters without much effort. For instance, if you own a blue T-shirt, you can Disney-bound as Stitch, the Genie, Dory, the Aliens from Toy Story, or Elsa. If you own a yellow T-shirt, you can Disney-bound as Pluto, Flounder, Belle, or Simba. The options are endless!

CHARACTER BAGS

The use of a kitschy purse or bag is my FAVORITE way to tell the story of a Disney character in ways the rest of an outfit can't. Your purse or backpack is usually the largest accessory you can wear, so it can work as your billboard, showing off a major character trait from

miles away. If your bag really articulates the character, you might not even need many other accessories to complete your outfit—it might do all the talking for you. I like to use bags that come in fun shapes, prints, patterns, or colors. It can be really useful if the bag evokes a sidekick, major plot point, or prop that your character comes into contact with on a regular basis. If you were creating a Disney-bound for Jack Skellington, the Pumpkin King . . . you would probably want to incorporate some sort of jack-o'-lantern detail, but you wouldn't want to carry one around. Instead, you could wear a jack-o'-lantern-shaped bag! And if you were working on a Disney-bound for Michael Darling, the youngest of the three Darling siblings in *Peter Pan*, you could wear a backpack shaped like a plush teddy bear. It tells the story of Michael without forcing you to carry an actual stuffed animal with you all day.

PLAYFUL JEWELRY

Jewelry is that cherry on top, the pièce de résistance of Disney-bounding basics. Items such as brooches, earrings, rings, necklaces, and bracelets are a good way to convey details from your character's storyline in a simple way, without the use of props. You can incorporate jewelry in the shape of animals, unique objects, or even weapons that are of importance to your character. If you were creating a Disney-bound for Thor, it wouldn't really feel like it was complete without his hammer, right? This is where jewelry really helps complete the design of your character. Don't worry about constructing a replica hammer from scratch—a quick Internet search brings up lots of options for Thor's hammer in the form of pendants and earrings. Unique brooches that you can wear on your lapel are another great way to finish off a Disney-bound for your favorite Disney character. If you were creating a Disney-bound for Robin Hood, that sly and lovable fox, and wanted to add in his iconic bow and arrow (without carrying weaponry with you to the mall), a collection of brooches might come in handy. Another search engine query brings up lots of options for bows and arrows in the form of brooches! It all depends on YOUR personal style and what jewelry items work with how you like to dress every morning.

You Don't Have to
Break the Bank

There are ways to Bound with any budget. This is a VERY important detail when it comes to the world of Disney-bounding. It's actually my favorite part about it. Disney-bounders come from all walks of life, with a variety of different budgets available to them. You shouldn't feel like you have to spend a lot. You might already have a few Disney characters hiding in your closet—maybe you've already thought of a few. I'll help you find these hidden gems a little later on in the book.

When it comes to Bounding on a budget, DIY is helpful! If you don't have an item, and you can't buy it . . . MAKE IT! The Disney-bounding community is full of some of the most creative people you'll ever meet. There is no limit to the endless ways they've found to create amazing Bounds with what's available to them.

You don't need to spend more than you can afford on yellow shoes. Why not make them instead? Do you have an old pair of white canvas shoes you never wear? They might be perfect for this project! If you don't have a used pair, check out bargain stores, which always have shelves stocked with simple white canvas shoes. Using fabric paint or dye, you can transform a pair of plain white canvas sneakers into the yellow shoes of your Disney-bounding dreams!

Remember that light-colored denim I told you to hold on to? Here is another great Disney-bounding DIY tip! Perhaps you want a pair of green jeans for your Peter Pan Disney-bound. Well, you can make them yourself! As long as the denim is light enough, you should be able to use fabric dye from a craft store. You can also do this with items whose silhouettes remind you of a Disney character, but that don't necessarily come in the right shade.

Craft stores are also full of great, affordable jewelry options. It just takes a little creativity and exploration! From pom-poms to charms, beads to yarn, you can use these items to design your own necklaces, bracelets, earrings, or brooches!

Never, ever, ever feel like you need to purchase every single item for a "look" in order to be dressed in your Disney-bounding best. If you're comfortable in what you're wearing and feel like your character inspiration is shining through, that's all that matters!

Now that you have the basics, let's find a way to incorporate each of these items into the perfect Disney-bounds for Mickey Mouse, Minnie Mouse, Donald Duck, Daisy Duck, and Goofy!

Mickey Mouse

In the words of Walt Disney himself, "I only hope that we never lose sight of one thing: that it was all started by a mouse." Starting this book with a Disney-bound for any other Disney character just wouldn't feel right. Mickey Mouse is a true icon and one of the most recognized characters in the world. This also rings true with Mickey Mouse Disney-bounds; Mickey's signature style

and colors are recognizable from miles away. Not only that, but Mickey-inspired outfits can be created with very little effort, so Mickey Mouse is always an easy and comfortable Bound to wear. It's perfect for those just starting out.

A Disney-bound for Mickey Mouse is all about the color blocking! When we take a look at him, the majority of his body is black, including his top half. His middle area is red, thanks to his red trousers, and his feet are yellow, thanks to his shoes. When building out a Disney-bound for any character, try to start the construction of your character by mimicking their color blocking. You can start creating this Mickey Mouse look by pulling your favorite black T-shirt out of your closet. A black T-shirt is a great staple to have. Red denim pants will also come in handy for this Disney-bound, as it's a simple way to match Mickey's

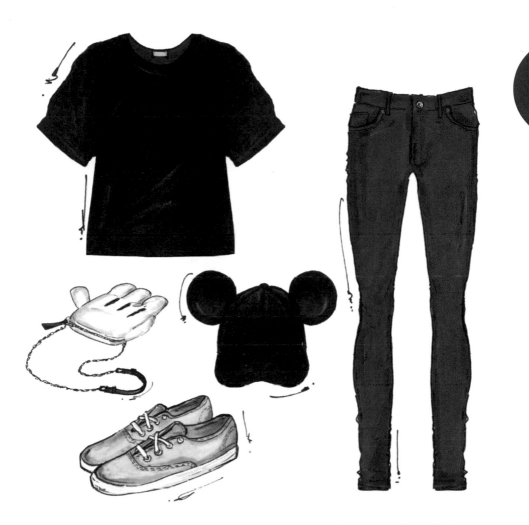

classic red trousers. Don't worry about re-creating the white buttons. Now for the yellow—it's all about those yellow shoes for Mickey Mouse! You could easily get the effect with a pair of bright yellow socks, too. Whichever way you choose to add your pop of yellow will be perfect.

If you want to take your Mickey Mouse Disney-bound up a notch, let's talk about accessories! The black silhouette of Mickey's head is a classic piece of Disney iconography that you will certainly want to re-create in some way

or another. One option that will take you down the more obvious route is wearing actual black mouse ears. An accessory I love that's available at many fashion retailers is a black baseball cap with his signature mouse ears on it. Alternately, you could go a more minimalistic route by wearing a simple pair of black Mickey Mouse–shaped earrings. There are lots of great Mickey Mouse–inspired accessories like this purse. Make sure you take some time to have fun exploring the ones that work best for you!

Minnie Mouse

Our girl Minnie Mouse is a fashion icon through and through! She has inspired many fashionistas around the world with her polka-dotted style, and she is never one to shy away from exploring new trends. She's been featured at New York Fashion Week and

even has her own star on the Hollywood Walk of Fame! Once again, start by exploring her blocked palette of colors. Unlike Mickey Mouse, her main color is red, with the added detail of the classic polka dots on her dress. This color and pattern can also be found between her iconic black ears in the form of a red-and-white polka-dotted bow. On her feet, you can once again find that Disney-bounding staple—yellow shoes!

Minnie's bow may as well be her logo. If you isolate the bow, even without the rest of her signature items, it still screams Minnie Mouse! So it's safe to say that a Minnie Mouse Disney-bound is not complete without adding that bow detail in there *somewhere*. The most obvious way to incorporate her bow

would be with an actual hair bow, but a hair bow is not necessarily something everyone can comfortably wear. This is where your personal style comes into play! For this look, I've used a bag with a bow accent on it, which is a way to mimic the bow without actually wearing one. If jewelry is more your thing, you can also try exploring all the licensed Minnie Mouse accessories that are available in Disney stores around the world. Things like Minnie-inspired necklaces, bracelets, and earrings are always easy to find, and can be a great way to add that extra spark to your look. There are many ways to put together a Disney-bound for the same character in a way that suits your personal style.

Donald
Duck

W e all know that Donald Duck is a bit of a cranky guy with an explosive attitude, but did you know that he's also quite the fashion guru? I bet you've never thought of him in that light, but his timeless nautical style is a look for the ages and can be taken in so many different directions. From va-va-voom vintage to fresh street style, Donald Duck is one of Disney's most underappreciated fashion icons.

In the spirit of fashion basics, let's keep this Disney-bound on the simpler side. When we take a look at the colors he's known for, blue is the primary one, falling on the top of his body and on his hat. He has a pop of red on his shirt in the form of a bow tie. Incorporating this color in your Disney-bound is a way to make sure your outfit goes from "nautical chic" to "definitely Donald." His feathers are white, and since he doesn't wear any pants, this leaves his feathered bottom half white as well. As for his legs and feet, they have a yellow-orange tone to them, which is where—you guessed it—those yellow shoes will really come in handy.

Rather than searching high and low to find the same unique blue sailor shirt that Donald wears, we can use a simple blue button-down shirt instead. (Don't feel like you have to limit yourself to

the pieces I'm suggesting. If you own a shirt similar to his, or are in the mood for hunting down that perfect piece, go right ahead!) For his bottoms, a pair of white chino pants re-creates his white feathers. If you want a Disney-bound with more detail, try exploring fun silhouettes and textures to emulate those feathers. Then lace up those handy yellow sneakers to create the tone on his legs and feet.

There are many ways to incorporate that pop of red in his bow tie. Begin by exploring the accessories that match your own style. For this Disney-bound, I used a bow tie similar to the one he wears—but if that's not your style, no problem. Perhaps you'd rather use a red hair bow, or maybe you're able to find a necklace with a red bow pendant. Some Disney-bounders will even re-create the look of a bow with sunglasses. At the end of the day, it's all about having that pop of red, not necessarily wearing the exact same thing Donald does.

Daisy Duck

Daisy Duck is one sassy, fashionable duck who is always serving up style, silhouettes, and accessories. From her puffy sleeves to her iconic hair bow, her pink stiletto pumps to the way her ruffled feathers resemble a skirt, Daisy is a fashion icon!

When we look at the color palette that makes Daisy Duck the piece of pastel perfection that she is, we notice that there are a few different colors that come into play. Daisy has a beautiful

shade of lavender on her midsection in the form of a puffed-sleeve blouse. Similar to Donald Duck, white ruffled feathers coat her bottom half, giving the illusion of a white skirt. (Keep this in mind; we'll play with that in a second.) She has pops of pink on the top and bottom thanks to her hair bow and pink pumps. There is also a pop of teal in the form of her teal bangle bracelet. Those are her iconic colors, and they are what you truly need to articulate that you're Disney-bounding Daisy Duck, so if you feel like omitting the yellow on her legs, go right ahead. Again, Disney-bounding is about what you feel comfortable in, so if you'd rather leave out a color or two in the spirit of your personal style, do it!

For this look, let's start with that lavender tone by using a simple purple T-shirt. It doesn't have to be the exact shade of purple. Disney-bounds are all

about the overall vibe that your outfit gives off, and not perfectly re-creating the character. For her bottoms—play around with silhouettes. By adding a few ruffles to your look (like the white skirt I've used), you give the illusion of white feathers.

Have a little fun with your accessories when you're creating your Disney-bound for Daisy. I used a block-heel sandal here, but heels certainly aren't the friendliest of shoes for a day at the Disney Parks. Make sure your shoes suit the occasion. Try pink high-tops or flats!

As we've explored with Minnie Mouse and Donald Duck, there are many ways to sport a bow. I've given this look Daisy Duck's classic pink hair bow in the form of pink cat-eye sunglasses—it's a way of creating the shape of a pink bow without actually using one. You can also go the more obvious route with a pink hair-bow headband. If you're more of the minimalist type, maybe your look will work best with a pink bow pendant or a pink handkerchief tied around your neck or hair.

Goofy

oofy is the king of layers! He's not one to shy away from pairing black with brown and a vest with a turtleneck, then topping it all off with a lime-green hat. On the surface it seems like a lot, but Goofy's style allows us plenty of room to play around with layering, giving us a lot to work with when we're creating a Goofy Disney-bound.

When it comes to Goofy, don't worry so much about accurately hitting every fashion detail that he wears. For your look, try focusing more on the general style Goofy presents us with instead. When we take a look at his layered color palette, we have a handful of tones to play around with. Around his midsection, he wears an orange turtleneck with a black vest layered on top—and the Parks' mascot version (in the photo) wears a yellow vest, which is another great option. On his bottom half, he wears blue jeans partnered with a pair of brown shoes. Topping off his crazy look is a bright green hat.

Yes, Goofy has a lot going on, but that doesn't mean your Disney-bound has

to. Make sure to play with layers that suit your style. This is a version of a Goofy Disney-bound that I personally would love to wear, but it's far from the only option. Instead of an orange turtleneck, I've used a simple long-sleeved orange shirt and then layered a fitted black faux-leather vest on top. I wanted to pay homage to the patches you sometimes see on his pants, so I've added in a pair of torn denim jeans. A Goofy watch is a fun but non-essential item.

Next are some trusty brown ankle boots. Finally, instead of going bright green with the hat, I've chosen a more subtle olive beanie. You don't always have to choose the exact colors that your character wears—if there are colors that are more complementary to your outfit or personal style, give them a try!

"Disney-bounds are all about the overall vibe your outfit gives off."

Chapter

2

The Importance of Accessories

Like with any fashion trend, accessories help complete your look.

Beyond their importance in the world of fashion, accessories play an important role when you put together your Disney-bound outfit. What is Mulan without a sword, Cinderella without a pumpkin, or Winnie the Pooh without a pot of honey? We've already talked a little about how you can use accessories to tell your character's story and incorporate key details that would otherwise be nearly impossible to bring out when you're visiting a Disney Park, or just hanging out with friends. You can get really creative with it! For instance, the bag you wear might actually be your sidekick, like one in the shape of a tiger for Rajah if you're planning on Disney-bounding as Jasmine. Or perhaps you might be able to use jewelry, like a necklace with a pendant in the shape of a frying pan for your Rapunzel Disney-bound. Your accessories fill in the blanks.

Disney-bounding is about YOU. You should never feel like you have to wear an accessory that you don't feel comfortable in. But you may find yourself using the added confidence you find through Disney-bounding to wear something a little outside your typical style. Disney-bounding adventures can help you uncover parts of yourself you didn't know existed, so don't limit yourself. Have fun and explore!

When it comes to fashion, I love breaking the rules (if you can't tell already). If you're drawn to Disney-bounding, I assume you feel that way, too! Still, there are rules that we do have to respect when we're visiting the Disney Parks or any public venue. Disney Park security is not too keen on visitors walking around dressed as Princess Leia with a replica blaster. They also wouldn't allow someone dressed as

Prince Phillip with a life-size sword through the gates. This is exactly where Disney-bounding comes into play. It gives you the opportunity to be creative with fashion. There are lots of ways to incorporate important aspects of your favorite Disney characters without using replica weapons or items you may not want to carry around in a social setting.

BAGS

We've already talked a bit about bags, so now let's talk about kitsch! Kitschy bags will quickly become your favorite accessory if you're planning on  diving deep into the world of Disney-bounding. They might be in the shape of animals, vehicles, or objects. They might use bright patterns, colors, or eye-catching fabrics. The definition of kitsch is "art, objects, or design considered to be in poor taste because of excessive garishness or sentimentality, but sometimes appreciated in an ironic or knowing way." That is exactly why I love bags with a level of kitschy detail to them. Disney-bounders know exactly how to appreciate this style because it's through this excess that they are best able to articulate their character. A bag can even play the role of another character separate from the one you're portraying.

DISNEY PINS

Disney Pins are not only great for trading! They have become the perfect cheap and easy Disney-bounding accessory, especially  for characters you might not be able to easily find accessories for. They are also a great way to add a little bit of character inspiration to your outfit without going too over the top, especially if accessories like jewelry and bags are not really your thing! If you're at a Disney Park, you might even be able to grow your Disney-bound throughout the day. Check out the pin trading stations to see if there are any pins that work even better for your Disney-bound than the ones you already have.

Ariel

Life will always be the bubbles when you're Disney-bounding Ariel! She is a very easy Disney-bound to recognize because her color palette is not commonly found in regular fashion. Her style is mer-mazing and can be interpreted in so many ways. Not to mention, she wears many outfits throughout her film, so if one of her looks doesn't speak to you, maybe another will! For now, let's take a look at her classic mermaid look.

She has three main colors when we break down the way she's color-blocked. There's the purple seashell bra around her midsection and the teal of her tail on bottom. She also has vivid red hair—and while that is an iconic detail, it's not a requirement. I'll get to that in a moment.

In lieu of a seashell bra, explore silhouettes that might pay homage to her shelled top. Perhaps you can go the crop top route if it suits your personal style. If you're more of a hoodie kind of person, you can take your Ariel Disney-bound in that direction! I've used a pair of teal shorts for her tail and gone with a lighter shade of mint for the sneakers, since her tail is a bit lighter on the bottom.

I'm not one to scream "less is more," but I understand that for many, the color combination of purple, teal, and red can feel a bit aggressive—and that's why red is not a necessity. You definitely don't have to worry about dyeing your hair red! Disney-bounding is more about fashion than it is about replicating the character. If adding a pop of red feels right for you, though, this outfit would look really cute with a red headband or hat!

Finally, for the bag, if you want something a bit more subtle, you could go with a pastel bag that matches one of the colors in the outfit. I like anything but subtle, so I've used a seashell-shaped bag. And, just to give a little extra detail, I chose a fork necklace and some cute character earrings. Another option is to include one of the friends who join her on her undersea adventure, like Sebastian or Flounder, with a bag in the shape of a crab or a fish!

Tiana

This Disney-bound will have us goin' down the bayou! *The Princess and the Frog*'s Tiana is another Disney character who would really rock a unique handbag. Like Ariel, Tiana has many possible outfits we can choose from. She might even have the most out of any Disney princess! From her yellow waitress outfit to her blue ball gown and even her bayou-chic bridal style, if you want to Disney-bound Tiana, you have many options available to you.

I think her most iconic and easily recognizable outfit is her green lily pad–inspired wedding gown. Her overall color palette is green, but each individual shade of green will play a role in building your Tiana Disney-bound. The primary shade on her gown is that gorgeous lily pad green, and that will be the main color we focus on.

Let's start this Disney-bound for Tiana with a lightweight dress—though you could also use a wrap playsuit. I chose this dress because the layered skirt gives the illusion of the lily pads on her gown. The frilly detail on top reminds me of the flowers and vines that decorate her bodice. To break up the green, let's include a pair of lemon yellow sandals that are similar to the shade found on the bottom of her skirt.

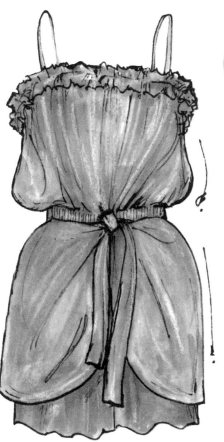

Have you ever noticed the turquoise necklace and earrings that Tiana wears? You can play around with that shade in the jewelry you choose—or you can exclude it entirely. It's all about your personal take on this frog princess! One very important detail I try to include in every Tiana Disney-bound I create is the lily flower on her waist. The way you incorporate this detail is entirely up to you. I chose to include a flower-shaped cocktail ring! If you feel you want to incorporate her crown, you could always add a gold headband as well.

As for that unique handbag to incorporate into your Tiana Disney-bound . . . I think there's one detail we haven't included yet, and that would be anything to do with a frog! Frogs play such a major role in this film that I want to make sure they get a bit more of the spotlight—which is why this frog handbag is the perfect addition!

Buzz Lightyear

To infinity and beyond! Buzz Lightyear is a character who really benefits from the inclusion of a backpack! You'll notice that he has a jet pack on his back at all times. From a silhouette perspective, there's a certain level of bulk that he carries back there. From a logistical perspective, you'll be able to store everything you need that day in your backpack!

Color-blocking Buzz Lightyear is a little bit more complicated than other characters we've looked at. This is where YOUR creativity will really come into play. If we take a look at his colors, we can see white, apple green, black, and purple. They each fall on him in a variety of ways, shapes, and placements. White is the bulk of his color palette, so that should also be your focus when creating a Disney-bound for him. Apple green ranks second and will make a great accent color. After those two tones, we see some purple, as well as a band of black around his waist. It's this breakdown that we will try to focus on the most. As always, your interpretation of him may be different from mine!

Usually, I'll start in the middle of a character and work my way out, but Buzz Lightyear is a special case. Instead, we'll work through each individual color. For this look, layer it up with a white denim

jacket and matching pants. That adds enough white to the Disney-bound. Since green is the second-most-common color found on Buzz Lightyear, let's use an apple green T-shirt. There's also a pop of green on Buzz's feet, and a pair of purple, green, and white sneakers seems fun! Now we need to add some more purple to this look. Notice his purple hood? Using a purple beanie would be a great way to incorporate that major pop of purple! One more important staple to include is a black belt, like the black band found around his midsection!

Remember when we talked about incorporating Disney pins into your Disney-bound? I purposefully selected a denim jacket because you can easily add a little flair to denim with enamel pins. A space ranger logo pin, similar to the emblem on his arm, is a great and subtle way to accessorize.

Instead of trying to go the more literal route and making a version of his jet pack, you can probably find a licensed Buzz Lightyear backpack online, or you could also wear a plain white, green, purple, or black backpack!

JEWELRY

As we mentioned in chapter one, jewelry is a great way to incorporate a wide selection of plot points and character details into your Disney-bound. It's especially great if you have a complex character who comes into contact with many different key items throughout their story, or if their story itself is a complicated one.

What I love the most about jewelry as a Disney-bound accessory is that there are so many budget-friendly options available. Just go online and you'll find a variety of stores with jewelry at different price points. With a simple web search, you'll be able to find dragon earrings that would be perfect for Mulan, or perhaps a magic lamp necklace for the Genie. If you search around, you're sure to find something without having to spend too much.

If you're not able to find jewelry that matches your character at a price point that works for you, *and* the incorporation of jewelry is important to you, this is where DIY jewelry comes into play. Set aside an afternoon and go on a jewelry exploration adventure at your local craft store. You'll find a great selection of charms, pendants, and even jewelry-making kits. Perhaps there will be something special that will perfectly suit that Disney-bound you're building!

GLASSES

Not every character requires glasses, but they are another great accessory for Disney-bounding!
This is where fashion frames really come into play. These frames may or may not have prescription lenses (depending on your optical needs). You can use them to add that finishing touch to give your Disney-bound added character context. As I demonstrated with Daisy Duck, glasses can complete an outfit even for characters who don't wear them. You can use glasses or sunglasses to give your Disney-bound that pop of color you're looking for, or to portray a detail like a bow, horns, or animal ears that you don't want to get too costumey with.

HAIR ACCESSORIES AND HAIRSTYLES

Playing around with hair accessories and hairstyles is a great way to help your Disney-bound go that extra mile. I encourage you to get creative with your hair, but don't worry about it looking exactly the way your character's does in the film. There are many ways that you can allude to the character you're Bounding through accessories or styling without creating a perfectly coiffed character wig.

When creating your Disney-bound, explore the large selection of on-trend hair accessories to see if any of them works for the character. Hair bows and hair ties are obviously fantastic for characters who wear them, but they are also great when you're trying to Disney-bound an animal with distinctive ears. The points on a bow can help create the appearance of cat ears, for example.

The way you style your hair can also add an extra level of character inspiration to your Disney-bounded outfit. With that being said, don't feel like there is only one way to style your hair in order to accurately portray your favorite character. There are many ways to style your hair, and this is an opportunity to really get creative and try something new! Everyone has different styling abilities, and everyone's hair is different—different amounts, lengths, colors, cuts, and textures. Whatever works for you is exactly the right way to do your hair, and never let anyone tell you otherwise. Use buns, braids, and curling or straightening irons to create a hairstyle that you feel represents your Disney character the best. A pair of buns will help you create bear or mouse ears, whereas a pair of pigtails is a great way to make bunny ears!

SCARVES

From a necktie to a beard, a scarf can be many things in the world of Disney-bounding.  Yes, you read that right: a beard. A scarf can actually play a really key role in communicating your Disney character inspiration to the rest of the world and create those extra details you might otherwise ignore.

Scarves can help take your Disney-bound to the next level, but they certainly aren't for everyone (or every climate). If scarves don't work for you, no problem! Keep your Bound about your personal style and expression of creativity!

Alice

When we look at Alice's color palette, it's simple—a combination of white and light blue, with a black bow in her hair and black shoes. She also wears an apron, but we don't need to incorporate this detail into our Disney-bound. Why not? Because if an apron isn't part of your usual wardrobe, why incorporate it now? You want to bring your own style to the table with Disney-bounding, so keep what you wear

100 percent you! Disney-bounding is about embracing your personal style through the love of Disney—so focus on your own style and not re-creating a character's costume piece for piece. Apron aside, her outfit is very layered. Inverting the color scheme and wearing a blue denim jumper dress or overalls with a white shirt is the perfect way to replicate the layering using your everyday wardrobe.

For her shoes, let's age up her outfit a little bit. Instead of using black Mary Janes, which might give a younger appearance to your Disney-bound, let's use white-and-black canvas sneakers, which give a similar color-blocking look. And perhaps hair bows aren't your thing? Instead of using a black hair bow, let's pull in sunglasses instead. With sunglasses, you're creating the

appearance of a pop of solid black, in a similar shape, placed in a similar area on the body. When you push them up on top of your head, it will be like you're wearing the black hair bow right where it belongs!

Alice comes into contact with many interesting characters, objects, and settings throughout her journey in Wonderland, which is why I think she's a great example of how to use jewelry and a kitschy bag in your Disney-bound!

From teacups to talking flowers, rabbits to hatters, queens to flamingos, there are so many options that the sky's the limit. With this huge list of props and characters, the choices are endless. Play around with different combinations of these characters and props to create your perfect *Alice in Wonderland* outfit. You can't really go wrong when you fall down the rabbit hole and start experimenting with fashion!

Merida

As a Disney fan, you've probably played the "Who is your favorite Disney Princess?" game. Well, for me, it's Merida. I love the way she breaks the rules of perfection that the other princesses seem to follow. There's something about her that is just so real. I can't tell you how many teal dresses

I own—I could probably Disney-bound Merida in about ten different ways based off the clothing I've stocked my closet with. Merida has two looks that you can Disney-bound. The first is her formal turquoise gown that's made from a satin material. The second look, and the one we are more used to seeing, is a dark teal/forest green gown with gold accents and brown leather accessories.

I created more of a party look here, but if you wanted to create a Disney-bound that she could run around the Scottish Highlands in, you could also use a teal playsuit as the base for this outfit. To accessorize the look, I've given her a brown belt and a pair of brown stacked heels. A pair of brown stacked-heel boots would look fantastic as well.

What do we do about the bears that play such a big role in her story? This is where a great kitschy bag will really come in handy. Let's top off this look with a black bear cross-body bag to pay homage to her mother (or Mor'du)!

And what's a curly-haired ginger princess without her bow and arrow, right? "A princess does not place her weapons on the table," according to Queen Elinor. A princess doesn't bring her weapon to public spaces where it may be frowned upon, either. Instead, let's give her arrow earrings and a bow necklace.

As I've mentioned before, it's not at all necessary to bring a character's hair color into your Disney-bound, but if you like headbands, you could add an orange one to this look.

Mr. Smee

I love a nautical look, and Mr. Smee knows how to work this style for the minimalists out there! His look can be really played up or comfortably worn with a few basics, depending on your personal style preference. I bet you've never stopped to think about what a stylish guy Mr. Smee is, have

you? Whatever your personal style, I bet there's a way that you can wear his look. Dress him up or dress him down! Not only is a Mr. Smee Disney-bound very versatile, it's also easy to create and comfortable to wear!

Start off by finding a blue horizontal-striped sweater or T-shirt and pair it with your favorite denim shorts. (His shorts are turquoise in the film, but blue shorts are much easier to find, and most people probably already have them in the closet.) Next, slip on a comfy pair of brown sandals. He wears a red beanie, but if you're visiting Orlando in July, you might want to opt for a different style of red hat, or omit it altogether. A red headband is another great way to top off this look.

While Mr. Smee is a pirate, the classic pirate accessories, which may

include skulls and crossbones or curved swords, don't really match his personal style. He is a much kinder and gentler pirate than his boss, Captain Hook. Since he gives off more of an overall seafaring vibe, why don't we include nautical accessories instead? I've included a pair of anchor earrings along with a white rope bracelet. There are lots of other nautical options out there for you to play with. Take a look at a few shops the next time you're visiting a beach town. You never know what Mr. Smee–style accessories are hiding there!

Finish off a Mr. Smee Disney-bound with his glasses. You can have a lot of fun with fashion frames, whether or not you have a prescription. Accessory stores at the mall offer a wide selection of frames that you can experiment with.

Rapunzel

We mentioned hair earlier, so let's create a Disney-bound for the lost princess and hair queen, Rapunzel! But before we discuss hair, let's talk about her dress. Her gown is a combination of purples and pinks, something that can be hard to find in your closet or at the local mall—so don't worry about being too technical and exact with her. From mauve to lavender, lilac to periwinkle, orchid to iris—there are so many different shades of purple that you can wear to create your Rapunzel Disney-bound. I found a lavender skater dress with a beautiful lace detail that reminds me of the details on the back of her gown.

Rapunzel spends most of her film running around barefoot. You, on the other hand, are going to need some shoes if you plan on leaving the house in your Rapunzel Disney-bound. Depending on the weather and your orthopedic needs, you can create the "barefoot" vibe with a pair of nude sandals or sneakers.

For her accessories, we have many options. Rapunzel comes into contact with a ton of unique objects and has many special moments throughout her

film. This allows you to really get creative with how you use accessories to portray her—just about as creative as Rapunzel gets when she's locked up in the tower. For the bag, let's use something really unique, like this painter's palette handbag that evokes one of her favorite hobbies. Rapunzel doesn't go anywhere without Pascal the chameleon, so I've included him in this outfit in the form of a chameleon cocktail ring. The golden sun motif is prevalent throughout the film, as it is symbolic of Rapunzel's

kingdom; I've added a pair of gold sun earrings.

Now, let's talk hair! You don't need to have blond hair that goes down to the ground to Bound like her. If you have longer hair that can be worn in a braid, do so! If not, you can just wear a smaller braid in the front. You don't even need a braid at all! Finish off the look with some flowers in your hair like the ones she wears. Then go out and enjoy your BEST. DAY. EVER!

Winnie the Pooh

This tubby little cubby all stuffed with fluff has the cutest style! From the yellow and red color blocking to the adorable accessories in the shapes of honey pots or bumblebees, you can always tell when someone is rocking a Winnie the Pooh Disney-bound.

There are many different ways you can interpret his style. He is simply color-blocked with yellow on top, red in the middle, and yellow on the bottom,

but you don't have to wear solid colors for a Disney-bound. I've started this Winnie the Pooh look with a pair of yellow gingham shorts. Gingham is a pattern that reminds me a lot of Winnie the Pooh because he loves his picnics, and that pattern is commonly used on picnic blankets. I've paired the high-waisted shorts with a red button-down short-sleeve shirt and finished off the basic outfit with our yellow shoes!

Choosing your accessories for Winnie the Pooh is easy. He's a simple bear who loves one thing more than anything else in the world, and that's HONEY! There's a great licensed Winnie the Pooh honey-pot bucket bag that's terrific for this look. Pooh wouldn't be complete without his honey pot! For the jewelry, I've paired this look with bumblebee earrings.

Now, what should we do about his ears? If you have hair long enough to be tied up into not one, but two topknots . . . give it a try! It's a cute and easy way to create bear ears. If you're a hat person, try a yellow bowler hat like the one here—the top of the hat kind of looks like Pooh's little bear ears!

Play around with Winnie the Pooh's colour blocking and love for all things honey. He's a character that can be easily identified through Disney-bounding from miles away so don't be afraid to really incorporate your own style into your Winnie the Pooh Disney-bound.

Thumper

Bambi's best friend, Thumper, is one Disney character who goes hand in hand with a cozy white circle scarf, don't you think? In order to create a Disney-bound for him, let's build him out with layers. Start with a tan dress, using a long gray cardigan layered on top. If this isn't your style, you can swap out the dress for a pair of gray jeans, a tan shirt and a gray cardigan—creating a similar vibe with a different style. As for shoes—don't Thumper's feet look like ballet flats? I think a pair of tan ballet flats is perfect for this look! You could play with a different style by wearing a pair of tan canvas sneakers instead.

They'll give a similar "bunny foot" appearance.

I've found a cute gray bag with rabbit ears that communicates this outfit's theme without the need to wear any kind of ears. You can pair the bag with a white faux-fur purse pom to

hint at your cotton tail—faux fur being the key detail in this ensemble.

To finish off your Thumper Disney-bound, let's add that white circle scarf I mentioned to replicate the extra bunny fluff he has on his chest! You can use other accessories to help complete your Thumper Disney-bound, from bunny pendant necklaces to flower earrings to symbolize the spring season in the film *Bambi*. There are a lot of cute, fun ways to top off your Thumper Disney-bound!

Grumpy

Never in a million years did I think I would be writing an excerpt on how to re-create a Dwarf's beard with accessories, but here we are! It's much more common than you might think, though. Lots of Disney-bounders will use a scarf to hint at a long beard. The Seven Dwarfs, Merlin, and King Triton are just some of the many bearded Disney characters that a scarf works great for!

The Dwarfs are very easy characters to re-create using items you can find in your own closet or at your local mall. They use a lot of button-down shirts, jeans or leggings, and beanies!

While there are Seven Dwarfs, let's focus on Grumpy! To start, grab a red button-down and a pair of fitted brown jeans. Tucking the shirt into the jeans with a French tuck will allow you to show off a black belt like Grumpy's. Each one of the Dwarfs wears a pair of booties, so I always like to mimic that detail with a comfy pair of ankle boots.

The Dwarfs all wear that classic wardrobe staple—the knit beanie. Beanies are great because they are easy to find in a wide array of colors.

Don't stress if you can't find that perfect shade—most people don't remember the exact colors that the Dwarfs wear anyway. Grumpy is an easy one, though, so top off the look with a brown beanie!

When it comes to jewelry for the Dwarfs, I try to think about what they would have access to. These guys don't care much about possessions . . . but they do have access to ample diamonds and gems. A pair of jeweled studs and a ring will help dress your Grumpy up a bit!

To finish off the Bound, add a white scarf around your neck to give yourself the bearded look.

Chapter
3

Personal
Style

Now, let's dig deeper into the most important part of a Disney-bound . . . YOU!

I believe in the importance of expressing your personal style at all times, so it's a mental challenge for me to write a book about fashion using only a handful of examples when there are infinite variations. My style may not be yours. Your style may not be the style of the person next to you. Personal style is one of the things in this world that always allows more room for discovery. Each new trend gives us the opportunity to explore it and make it our own.

This goes for Disney-bounding as well. Never feel like there is only one way to do it right. Each and every Disney character is open to YOUR interpretation. In fact, your unique view of each character is your contribution to the Disney-bounding community! You may pick up on a detail that others have not—or you might express their style in a way that no one has before. Trends are set by those who aren't afraid to be different and express themselves, and each and every one of you has the opportunity to be a trendsetter in this community. Remember, long before anything becomes "on trend," someone has to start it.

Which Characters
Already Live in Your Closet?

I always encourage those just getting into Disney-bounding to look through their closets before they go shopping. You never know what Disney characters are hiding away in there. Here are a few tips and tricks that will help you create characters out of what you already own!

1. Look at the color that appears the most in your wardrobe. If you have a lot of black, maybe start with a Disney villain Disney-bound. Ursula, Maleficent, Cruella De Vil, and Yzma all love wearing black! If you have a lot of blue denim, Stitch, Fix-It Felix, or the Genie would work!

2. Look for the pieces that stand out. Perhaps they have a unique silhouette that reminds you of a particular character, even if they aren't the right color. There might be a way to incorporate those items into a Disney-bound in the future.

3. Set aside your colored jeans! If you've got red pants, you're already a third of the way to an easy Mickey Mouse Disney-bound. If you have green pants, you're not too far away from creating Peter Pan!

4. Do you have any unique bags? Perhaps they are a fun shape or color . . . or even have a Disney character printed on them. A bag is a great way to finish off a Disney-bound!

5. Any and all jewelry pieces or accessories can be useful when creating a Disney character. Even a simple gold tennis bracelet could come in handy for any character who might benefit from a little pop of gold, like Merida, Prince Charming, or Jasmine!

Like most Disney-bounders, you want to express yourself through your fashion, and your personal style is your calling card—it's your identifier. When you're not afraid to be exactly who you are, you can introduce yourself to a room before you even say your name. And this is where Disney-bounding gets really fun. If you walk in a room and you're Mickey Mouse, you're telling the world you're an original—you're the star. When you walk into a room and you're Cinderella, that day you are royalty! It's all about who you feel inspired by on that particular day!

Mulan

Many Disney characters wear multiple outfits throughout their film, so while one outfit may be hard to replicate or might not feature colors you feel comfortable wearing, there might be another way you can Disney-bound as them, by focusing on one of their other outfits. Mulan is a great example of this!

One of Mulan's most iconic looks is her Matchmaker dress. This look features a lot of pinks and purples and benefits from a lot of floral accents. It's important when creating a Disney-bound for Mulan that we are respectful of the Chinese culture and don't use their traditional costumes as fashion. So, how do we create the vibe of a *hanfu* with the clothes we can find in our own closet? With a lot of layering!

For this look, I'm going to start color-blocking in the middle, since that's where it can be the trickiest. The primary color around her waist is a beautiful royal blue, secondary to a cherry red tone. Let's use a blue T-shirt to create the "around the waist" tone, and if you

have one, you could even use a skinny red belt to mimic hers. The color we see the most in this look is a cherry blossom pink, so let's use a long pink cardigan to give a similar silhouette. For the bottom, I've added a raspberry denim skirt, similar in color to the shade that falls towards the bottom of her hanfu.

Since Mulan's conversation with her father under the cherry blossom tree is one of the most memorable scenes featuring this look, I've found the perfect pair of pink sneakers with cherry blossoms printed on them. Her guardian, Mushu, is never too far away, so I've given her a dragon necklace.

Mulan as Ping

When Mulan was called to a greater adventure, we watched her transform into Ping, a warrior who could enroll in the military and ultimately save China from the Huns.

Mulan's warrior outfit is one that also gives us a lot of layers . . .

too many layers. It would be hard to perfectly re-create this look without wearing about four layers. Layers are usually my go-to answer for building out details without getting too costumey, but for this look, let's scale back . . . a lot. To start off this outfit, I like to look at the shape of her black armor. It's almost like a T-shirt, so let's start with a simple black tee.

She wears a lot of different greens, and they are greens that are not always easy to find in the mall. Feel free to play around with the shades of green that are readily available to you and don't worry too much about accuracy. I know olive green is usually available, so let's layer the black T-shirt with an olive green military jacket. While it's a different style from what she wears,

the military aspect gives the outfit a warrior vibe. I tried to find a shade of green pants that matched the green jacket, but in a slightly different tone, since she wears multiple greens. The black canvas shoes that I used remind me of hers—they have the two-toned aspect with black and white.

For those with hair long enough to throw into a bun, I've included a green hair tie similar to the one she wears. A sword is an obvious prop that goes hand in hand with saving China, but let's swap that out for a sword necklace instead.

However you decide to create your Mulan Disney-bound, make sure it's something that you feel comfortable in. Let your creativity shine through!

Be Yourself,
Whoever You Are

While there may be a distinct way to rock a certain fashion trend . . . there is no wrong way to express your personal style. That's the beauty of it all. There is literally no wrong way to be yourself. Your personal style is your fingerprint in the world of fashion—there is no other quite like it. In a world where we're often expected to fall in line, how you dress is one way that you never have to do the same thing as someone else, and no one can fault you for that. In fact, some might even celebrate the disorder you choose to bring to a look. There is nothing wrong with a little fashion anarchy.

Sometimes it's hard not to compare ourselves to others, but it's important to know that there is no one out there quite like you. Each and every time you dress the way you want to dress, you are expressing a very deep and

personal part of yourself and showing it off to the world. Don't be afraid to step out in something that is all your own—regardless of what others around you are wearing.

Even within a group of friends, it's okay to be different . . . it's okay to be you. Take a moment and think of your closest friends. Do you think the exact same things they think in a day? Do you do the exact same things they do? Eat the exact same things they eat? There is a 99.9 percent chance that your answer to those questions is no. So why would you feel like you have to wear the exact same things they do? By giving yourself that freedom to express yourself uniquely through fashion, even in a group of friends who may do everything together, you are allowing yourself to let go, and you can truly be who you are meant to be.

Explore Your Personal Style

I know it's hard for many to think of themselves as stylish . . . but I'm here to tell you that EACH and EVERY ONE of you is stylish. Fashion is only an outer layer; style is something personal that lives deep inside of us. The way to truly feel stylish is by feeling good in what you wear. The way to feel good in what you wear is by wearing the clothes that express who YOU are. As trends come and go, your personal style will ALWAYS stay with you. Explore it. Grow it. Let it take the lead and guide you as you put your Disney-bound together. Don't worry about what others might say.

I know that for many, the concept of stepping away from a subdued "everyday look" into a Disney-bounder's wardrobe may be a scary thing. I often say that you can spot Disney-bounders at a Disney Park just by looking for a group of really colorful people. But if color isn't your thing, that's okay! There are a lot of Disney characters out there who have quite muted color schemes—you don't have to be a Flit if your personal style is more Meeko. However, that being said . . . maybe Disney-bounding will encourage you to step outside your comfort zone, and you'll try something new—be it a color, a silhouette . . . or maybe even a Disney character you don't know much about.

Don't be afraid to stand out! You could be that little extra touch of Disney magic someone needed in their day!

While I and the rest of Disney-bounding community welcome and encourage the expression of personal style and the creativity that grows from it . . . some others may be threatened by it, but don't let that stop you. Personal style can be threatening to some because it means you aren't following the rules. Sometimes society sends the message that rules must be followed, and those who don't are weeds that must be picked. You aren't a weed. You're a wildflower who is meant to blossom! In the Disney-bounding community, you will be blossoming next to many other wildflowers. Never allow anyone's negative perceptions change how vibrantly you bloom. Be bright, be colorful, be unique.

Aladdin

There are so many different ways to style a Disney character. However you decide to build your Bound will be the right way—you can't do it wrong. Aladdin is a great example of this.

Let's have a little fun with the first Aladdin look! This outfit will be perfect for the Disney-bounder who loves to take an

outfit in a bohemian direction. To mimic his bare chest without going shirtless, I've layered a tan crop top under a purple fringed vest. To replace his white parachute pants, let's use a pair of white denim shorts. By using denim, we are able to wear a red belt like his! As for his fez? Let's go with a wide-brimmed red fedora to really amp up the boho-chic style. Since he runs around barefoot, we'll keep the ankle boots a tan tone as well!

For accessories, let's think of the items he comes into contact with the most! We'll definitely need to make sure Abu is part of this look, so I've added a ring with a cute little monkey on it. The bag I selected reminded me of the Magic Carpet, and it matches perfectly with the red tones. As for the necklace, I found the perfect magic lamp pendant.

Maybe boho chic isn't your style. That's no problem! There are so many ways that you can rock any Disney character! Let's keep the next look simpler.

Maybe creating a faux-bare chest isn't really what you'd call "fashion," and a simple purple tee is more up your alley. Combine your T-shirt with your favorite pair of white trousers so that you'll feel comfortable all day! Add a red belt to your look, and see if you can find your favorite style of shoes in tan to create that barefoot vibe. If you're not a hat person, throw on a pair of red-framed sunglasses. They'll keep your eyes protected from the sun while giving the same pop of red we need.

See? There are many ways to dress as any Disney character, so don't forget to make it your own. It's what you're most comfortable in that truly matters.

"Every Disney character is open to YOUR personal interpretation."

Chapter 4

Tips and Tricks

While some folks in the fashion world like trends to stay within the lines, I LOVE coloring outside the lines (literally).

I love to encourage Disney-bounders to create a Bound that suits them, no matter how many style rules they have to break! That's what makes the community so amazing. But there's a difference between breaking the rules of fashion and breaking the costuming rules put in place by a private space that welcomes you onto the property. For more information on the rules of the Disney Parks, please check the official Disney website.

Here are some tips and tricks that will help you incorporate certain costumey aspects into your outfit without actually wearing a costume!

Weapons and Props

What's Thor without his hammer? Or Han without his blaster? When dressing like your favorite Disney character, it's hard to feel like your look is complete without their iconic weapons or other props that play a big role in their stories. But many public spaces have rules about carrying props and fake weapons—and for obvious reasons, this includes the Disney Parks.

This is where Disney-bounding REALLY shines, because there are lots of ways you can incorporate these pieces without requiring their presence in a physical form. Using Mulan as an example, let's explore accessory options to complete your look without using an actual sword. If jewelry is your thing, look online for a sword pendant or a ring with a sword accent. If your style is more vintage, maybe you can find a sword in the form of a brooch.

Capes

In the words of the Disney fashionista Edna Mode, "NO CAPES!" Guests are not allowed to wear capes at Disney Parks. This is no problem for Disney-bounding, though! There are lots of ways to give your outfit a caped effect without putting on something that drags on the floor.

My go-to is always a long cardigan or a zip-up hoodie that you can wear over the rest of your outfit. This layered effect gives the impression of a cape without wearing one. If it suits your style, you could even give your outfit more of a preppy inspiration and tie a cardigan around your shoulders. Sometimes, you can just omit the cape and your character's personality will come shining through regardless. Characters like Elsa

or Mother Gothel do wear capes from time to time, but it's not an accessory that defines their appearance.

The Queen from *Snow White* is a great example of a character who needs a cape to create her look. Her long black cape often hides the purple gown she wears underneath. To create a Disney-bound for her, let's start with a purple romper! She is a queen, after all, so use gold accessories to give her a regal look. I've used a gold crown ring for this Disney-bound.

Layer the romper with a long black cardigan. This will take the place of a cape to give your outfit some movement as you walk around the park (although it would be an awful lot of fun to whip a long black cape around every corner of Magic Kingdom Park).

I know some of you must be reading this thinking, "A cardigan? In Orlando? Are you crazy?!" Comfort and confidence should ALWAYS come first. If the character needs a cape but the heat of Hong Kong, Orlando, or Anaheim is telling you otherwise, consider a backpack that matches the color of the cape. This will allow the color to fall on your body where it falls on the character, without your melting into a puddle in Epcot.

Elsa

I love a snow queen with a beautiful long cape! But when it comes to the wear and tear that any outfit goes through in a day, it might be better to leave your cape at home—especially if you're heading to the Disney Parks, where capes that drag on the ground are not allowed. Instead of wearing a long snowflake cape, you could use a light blue cardigan with a similar flow and flair to it. The general theme of her look is blue with a little extra sparkle, so however you interpret that combo depends on how you feel that day.

Elsa can be Disney-bounded in a few ways. Her gown is made out of gradients of blue, so if you wanted to take it up a notch, explore this patterning in your Disney-bound. I used an ombré dress with a white pattern that reminded me of snowflakes. You can also explore a wide array of blues for this look, even if they don't perfectly match the blues that appear in Elsa's outfit. For instance, you could wear lighter shades on top and then darker shades on the bottom.

Don't forget to have a little fun with the accessories! I imagine that Elsa would enjoy a little sparkle, don't you? She's a snow queen, after all, so when you're exploring accessories for her, play around with the tones, textures, and shapes of what she would come in contact with the most: ice and snow! I picked a glittery boot and snowflake jewelry, but you could also use a snowflake pendant, or some crystal earrings—whatever adds a little extra sparkle to your Elsa Disney-bound.

Wigs

One of the best parts of Disney-bounding is that looking like the character is not a requirement—it's all about expressing your love for the character through fashion. And it doesn't matter what your hair looks like. Cinderella can have black hair, Mulan can have curly hair; this is your chance to make your favorite character YOU!

That's not to say that you can't wear a wig with your Disney-bound. Lots of people rock wigs on the daily for personal or medical reasons—or just as a way to have fun with their style.

However, when you're taking your Disney-bound to the Disney Parks, leave your character wig (a wig styled to look exactly like a character's hair) at home. If you replicated a character to a T, you might be confused for an official park character, and that's not safe for the characters or other guests.

Don't worry—there are other options you can explore. Take Merida, for example. Her fiery, curly red hair is a major part of her look, but instead of grabbing a curly ginger wig, use hats or hair accessories to add in that pop of orange. If your hair cooperates with styling, try adding a few ringlets or just rocking your natural curls! It doesn't matter if it matches her shade; Merida's vibe will still stand out with the outfit you create!

Some Disney characters, like Alice, Tiana, and Belle, wear aprons as part of their looks. However, to keep your Disney-bound from looking too much like a costume, the apron is one detail you might have to get a little creative with. You probably don't wear an apron to school, the mall, or the Disney Parks, right? That's why we can avoid this detail when putting together our Disney-bound for a character who has an apron.

There are ways to incorporate the idea of an apron into your Disney-bound without grabbing one from your kitchen. Belle, for example, has a layered look with a white blouse under a blue pinafore dress and a white apron on top. To create the layered look, I will often go with a blue denim jumper dress or overalls—but you can omit the layering entirely and just go for something blue. With all the accessories involved, your character inspiration will usually come shining through without using an apron at all.

Chapter 5
Bounding Around the World

T

the bulk of the Disney-bounding community is located in North America, but thanks to the reach of social media, there are Bounders ALL OVER THE WORLD!

It's a small world after all, right? Each country brings a unique take to the movement. Fashion trends are different around the world, and it's fun to see how a trend is interpreted as it spreads across the globe.

For instance, in Europe, where Disneyland Paris is their main park, Disney-bounders tend to go for a more classic fashion interpretation. In Tokyo, where matching with your friends is very trendy, it's not uncommon to run into a group of Ariels all wearing the same thing.

The year that Shanghai Disneyland opened, I gave myself the incredible challenge of traveling the world and seeing all the Disney Parks in one year. This includes Disneyland, Walt Disney World, Disneyland Paris, Tokyo Disneyland, Hong Kong Disneyland, and Shanghai Disneyland. I managed to not only conquer the goal—but I was lucky enough (or crazy enough, depending on how you look at it),

to do it all in three months . . . and I even made a visit to Aulani, Disney's Hawaiian resort on the island of Oahu, just outside Honolulu.

With each park visit, I made sure to put together a Disney-bound that matched one of the unique themes found at that park. There was something so special about being able to Disney-bound around the world. No matter what language we speak, Disney fans around the world know what their favorite characters look like. So you can be in Hong Kong and still get your Disney-bound recognized. It's so much fun!

When people find out that I've been to every Disney property in the world, they always want to know which one is the best. My honest answer? They each have something unique about them that makes visiting worthwhile! Don't assume that just because you've been to one, you've seen them all.

In this chapter, let's travel the world together.

I'm going to take you to each major Disney property around the globe and share some tips and tricks, as well as suggest a special Disney-bound for each spot.

Aulani, a Disney Resort & Spa

Disney's Aulani is a little patch of Disney paradise just outside of Honolulu.

I think the thing I love the most about this property is how incredibly relaxing it is. I often forget to take breaks in life, but Aulani does a great job of giving you no other option. I tell everyone who goes to make sure they visit the spa—it is easily one of the best spas I have ever been to!

I find that Disney-bounders like to plan their outfits based off photo settings or characters they might meet. At Aulani, you'll be able to meet all the classics—with a twist! Mickey, Minnie, Donald, Daisy, and Goofy wander the property in Hawaiian resort wear. Goofy even goes in the water (up to his knees) when he leads the afternoon pool party! Pro tip: If you want to match their outfits, you'll have a lot of luck at beach shops in Honolulu! On my last visit to Aulani, I was driving down from the North Shore and dropped into a beach shop to grab water. Suddenly, right in front of me was THE PERFECT dress for a Bound of Minnie Mouse's Aulani resort wear. I bought it in a heartbeat, and Minnie was very excited to see that someone was dressed just like her.

You'll also get to meet some characters that are very popular in Asian countries. Duffy and ShellieMay can be found roaming the property in their resort wear as well!

Don't forget to find Stitch while you're there. If you don't happen to cross paths with him, there is a Stitch totem on the property that is a great place to pose in your *Lilo & Stitch* Disney-bound!

However, I think my favorite Polynesian Disney-bound to wear is Moana! Walk down the beach at Aulani out to the grassy peninsula. That's the perfect spot for a Moana photo op!

Moana

After a fun day of sunbathing and exploring Waikolohe Valley, Aulani's water park, it's the perfect time to slip into your Moana Disney-bound for your dinner reservations before checking out the Ka Waʻa Lūʻau!

I started off this look by trying to find an off-the-shoulder top in the same color as hers. There's no need to nitpick the shade of her top—it's a hard one to replicate, but it also blends well with so many other shades. Whether your shirt is salmon, orange, red, or something in between, your outfit will still read as Moana overall. To get the same vibe as her grass skirt, I pulled on a pair of cream crochet shorts and paired this look with a woven grass clutch! Moana's outfit also has an orange belt that matches her top. This is one of those situations where you don't necessarily need to add every detail that you see on the character. In this outfit, a belt isn't needed, so I've left it out. Perhaps in

your Disney-bound outfit, a belt makes sense. While Moana is barefoot in her film, there are many spots at Aulani where you can't go barefoot—so I've added a pair of nude sandals to give as little focus to the feet as possible.

When you're visiting these amazing spots around the world and Bounding as your favorite characters from that region, it's important that you don't borrow cultural aspects to make your Bound more "accurate." Accuracy is not the goal—Disney-bounding is all about having fun while also remaining respectful to those around you. For Moana's necklace, I purchased a turquoise stone necklace created by a local artist as a way to support the island and those who have lived on it for many generations! There are many other character details you could also add to your Disney-bound outfit. A ring, bracelet, or earrings that feature a pig or a rooster would be the obvious choices. Perhaps you could include a stingray charm for Gramma Tala!

Disneyland Resort

Welcome to the place where it all began!

When you're visiting the Disneyland Resort, you can feel the history unfolding before your eyes. There is so much of this park that has been touched by Walt Disney himself, and that's what makes the experience so incredibly special for the guests who are visiting.

Because I'm someone who hangs out at theme parks quite a bit, you might be surprised to know that I'm actually terrified of roller coasters. But that's the beauty of the Disney Parks: there are plenty of rides that everyone can go on, so you really get the full experience, whatever your coaster tolerance level is.

It's hard to pick my favorite thing to do on the Disneyland side of the park. Adventureland and Frontierland are easily the lands I like best. Indiana Jones™ Adventure is a ride that you can't find anywhere else in the world— and it's also my favorite ride in the park.

There's nothing quite like Cars Land on the Disney California Adventure side of the park. That moment when you're walking down the road and suddenly Lightning McQueen is driving right in front of you is indescribable! And if you're a Motown fan like me, head over to Flo's for a bite to eat. The soundtrack there is on point! So let's get you ready for a visit to Radiator Springs, shall we?

Lightning McQueen

Now . . . how do you dress like a car? Great question. Lucky for you, this is the kind of weird stuff I live to figure out. Unlike a human, where the clothing items are a bit more obvious and may be taken more literally, dressing like a car is really more open to interpretation! There are a few ways that I've seen Lightning McQueen

Disney-bounded. Some of the looks are more literal, whereas others will incorporate car-related details, like the black-and-white checkers of a racing flag, to break up all the red.

When I'm putting together a Bound for a character who is basically one solid color, I like to use a dress, romper, jumpsuit, jumper dress, or overalls to minimize the feeling of wearing too many items that are the same color. This also makes it easier to ensure that you don't have to match the different reds of a bunch of different items to each other. So, for this Bound of Lightning McQueen, let's use a fun pleather romper. I like playing around with textures and fabrics for the Cars characters, since there are so many

wearable fabrics (patent leather, suede, metallics, etc.) out there that are similar to something you'd find in an actual car.

I chose a pair of black boots with a chunky rubber heel and a bit of texture on the sole of the shoe—doesn't it kind of remind you of a tire? Since it's his namesake, an accessory with a lightning bolt is a must-have for Lightning McQueen—I used a belt. I also added a necklace with a Lightning

McQueen charm; it's a fun addition, but not needed. To finish off the look, I was able to find these toy car tire earrings. Dressing like a car is kind of fun, isn't it?!

This outfit has a visit to Disney's California Adventure written all over it! There are so many photo ops in Radiator Springs that are calling your name!

Walt Disney World Resort

I love visiting Walt Disney World because of its size.

It's SO big that you can visit the park every year of your life, and your trip will never be the same twice. There are so many ways to take in the sights and sounds of this park.

Has a Disney ride ever brought you to tears? For me, that's the new Avatar Flight of Passage at Disney's Animal Kingdom! It's an incredible experience. There is a sense of freedom on this ride that is unlike anything in the real world. If you're able to make your way over to Animal Kingdom during your next visit, don't miss the chance to experience this sense of freedom for yourself!

Have you ever taken a day to go resort-hopping? Each resort hotel—including the value resorts—has its own spots to explore and unique restaurant menus. The next time you visit, try to make a meal reservation at a resort you haven't visited before! It's a perfect chance to experience the parks in a new way.

At Walt Disney World, the Disney-bound options are endless! There are tons of great backdrops, whether you visit a resort that matches the character you're Bounding or happen to find the perfect locale in the park. Epcot is one of those great places where you can find the perfect photo op for just about any Disney character on the roster!

One Disney character who does not get enough love is Figment, though he does have a devoted group of fans who get excited every time they see him. He is a special little purple-and-orange dragon who can be found on the Journey Into Imagination ride at Epcot. So let's journey into imagination together and create a Disney-bound of Figment for your next visit to Epcot!

Figment

I absolutely love Figment's color scheme! He is a brilliant combination of lavender, bubblegum pink, and sunny orange—it's a fun Bound to put together. When a character has a two-toned body like Figment does, I like to work with layers.

Let's start off with a pink skater dress to replicate the tone on his stomach. For the purple, let's keep our layering light with a lavender chiffon cardigan, since it's pretty likely that it will be hot when you're visiting Walt Disney World.

I've learned the hard way that it doesn't matter how cute the shoes you want to wear for a day at Walt Disney World are. If you think they might be uncomfortable . . . they will always be *way more* uncomfortable than you ever expected. You will be doing a lot more walking than you think. That's where a pair of lavender sneakers comes in handy. They will look cute with your outfit and won't ruin your feet in the process. That said, even these shoes are not for everyone. Never ruin your Disney

vacation in the name of fashion. Wear what is comfortable for you!

For Figment's horns, I've added a pair of orange sunglasses. Not only will they protect your eyes from that incredible Floridian sun, but when you push them up onto your head when you're inside, they will be in the same place as his horns!

This little purple dragon isn't complete without his orange wings, so I've found a pendant with an orange wing.

However you decide to imagine your Bound, feel free to be extra playful. After all, nothing is more Figment-like than creativity and outside-the-box thinking!

Disney Cruise Line

If you haven't had the opportunity to take a Disney Cruise, I highly recomment you bump it to the top of your Disney vacation bucket list!

If you feel like you're not a cruise person, I am your firsthand evidence that YOU ARE! I am pretty open about my anxiety, so to say that I'm a chicken is an understatement. The idea of being in a small space on a boat, while being in a big wide-open space in the ocean, was enough to make me weak in the knees. And then . . . I stepped onto a Disney Cruise.

From the moment you enter the ship and the entire staff cheers your arrival—yes, they actually do this!—you become immersed in the Disney Cruise experience. I've already mentioned that relaxing is not my strong suit, but a Disney Cruise is another place where relaxing is encouraged! I can't stress this enough—don't spend your first day trying to do EVERYTHING. When I went on my first cruise, we had an "explore it like you explore Walt Disney World" mind-set. We saw almost everything there was to see on the first day and then realized, "Oh, I guess we have more time than we thought." You will have time to do it all, so take your time and enjoy it. Relax! When you're out at sea, you'll have nothing to do but explore the ship!

My very FAVORITE part of a Disney Cruise is Pirate Night. For those who don't know what this is, it's a post-dinner event where you're encouraged to dress up as a pirate and head to the top deck for a special show and dance party. The energy on the boat shifts—everyone has been spending the day doing their own activities, and now the entire ship is taking part in this event together. The speakers in the hallway play pirate-y Disney tunes, and before you know it, you're running into more pirates than you are fellow shipmates. I've put together a Hook Disney-bound that would be perfect for Pirate Night—just turn the page!

Adventures by Disney

I have been obsessed with Adventures by Disney for years!

It's an incredible Disney travel company that offers a wide array of excursions around the world. An Adventures by Disney trip allows you to travel the world through the eyes of Disney—and experience the same quality you get when you visit a Disney Park.

The excursions I'm most drawn to are the ones that take you on an adventure in a country that is home to a Disney character. Imagine journeying through the Scottish Highlands, Disney-bounding as Merida . . . or exploring the ruins of ancient Greece in an outfit inspired by Hercules. Adventures by Disney and Disney-bounding are really a great match. They both represent a way to have a touch of Disney magic outside of a Disney Park.

With so many incredible excursions to choose from, it's hard to select only one for our Disney-bounding adventure, but one does stand out in my mind—and in Anna's, too! Let's go to Norway on page 90. . . .

Captain Hook

All aboard your Disney Cruise! You'll want to make sure you're prepared for all the fun and games that the Disney Cruise Line cast members have prepared for you. You'll know Pirate Night is about to begin as the music playing in the hallway begins to take on more of a scallywag tone! You'll receive some pirate-inspired accessories in your cabin before Pirate Night begins so that you can participate even if you didn't bring anything, but let's take your Pirate Night outfit up a notch with a Disney-bound dedicated to Captain Hook!

I wanted to create a look that was ready for an evening out on a Disney Cruise while still being easy to wear—it's your vacation, after all! This look can easily go from dinner to the pirate-themed activities so you don't even have to go back to your cabin to change if you don't want to. Let's start with a white blouse that features a light ruffled detail on the chest. If ruffles aren't for you, that's no problem! A plain white shirt will work as well. Layer up the look with a red blazer, like one Captain Hook might wear.

His trousers are a pinkish-purple shade, but any color from red to black will also work. While I love a great color clash, it's not everyone's cup of tea! Your Disney-bounds can be as loud or muted as you'd like them to be. If you can find a wide-brimmed fedora in the same shade, it will help your outfit read as Captain Hook. Wrap up the main pieces by adding a pair of black boots with a buckle detail!

What about his hook? You can't have Captain Hook without it! You don't need to actually cart a fake hook hand around with you—I used a necklace with a hook charm. Remember, your Disney-bound doesn't need costume accuracy. You're creating a vibe with your outfit, not a replica. To finish off the look, I added a crocodile ring to pay homage to the Tick Tock Croc!

Anna

The younger of the two Frozen sisters, Anna, may have been a princess, but she's always been the queen of color blocking, and that's why I love creating Disney-bounds for her. Her Bound really doesn't require much detail beyond her colors.

Norway isn't known for its tropical temperatures, but that's okay; Anna is all about the layers! Not only will playing with layers help you create an accurate representation of her outfit, but it will also keep you warm as you're exploring Norway on your Adventures by Disney excursion. This look will be perfect for a day of adventuring through fjords and medieval churches!

Let's start with her top—this is where less is more. You could layer a long-sleeved mint cardigan over a black shirt, but you really don't have to. Just a black shirt does the trick!

You probably don't want to wear a skirt on your big Adventures by Disney trip, so let's swap hers out for a pair of embellished jeans. I like the added decoration here because her skirt features a beautiful floral design. It's those little details that bring that extra flair to your outfit. For your footwear, you

want to be ready for whatever the day throws at you, so a pair of black boots will be perfect. Keep yourself warm with a fuchsia jacket to stand in for the cape Anna wears! If you'll be inside for most of the day, you can opt for an oversized pink cardigan in lieu of a jacket.

In terms of accessories—she doesn't really need very much. I always like to give her a pair of snowflake earrings to pay homage to the emotional journey she goes on with Elsa! Gold is a big accent color for Anna, so I stick with gold-toned metals. To take your Disney-bound to the next level, throw your hair in a pair of braids—or add a little braided accent to your hair if it's not long enough to braid in full.

Disneyland Paris

T hose who are accustomed to warmer temperatures may disagree, but my favorite time to visit Disneyland Paris is in the winter—December to be specific.

I'm Canadian, so I'm not afraid of a little snow, but what a unique experience it is to visit a Disney Park and find snow on the ground. It's not incredibly cold or anything ("Yeah, right," says every Floridian reading this book), but it will give you an opportunity to wear that cute winter coat that's been sitting in your closet but never comes with you on a Disney vacation.

If you're a *Peter Pan* fan, you'll want to pack a Peter Pan Disney-bound, because they actually have a huge pirate ship and Skull Rock over in Adventureland. You'll be able to pose across the pond from it for that perfect photo op. Or perhaps you're a big *Alice in Wonderland* fan! Get lost in Alice's Curious Labyrinth and take a few pictures while you're there.

There is no greater backdrop than La Place de Rémy, the *Ratatouille* area in Walt Disney Studios Park. It's a unique spot with many small details that any fan of the film will love to explore!

Remy

Keeping with the winter theme, let's put together a Bound for Remy that will be perfect for the colder temperatures of a wintertime visit to Disneyland Paris! Experiencing a Disney Park in the snow is such a special experience, and you're unlikely to get it anywhere else. Creating a Bound for colder weather is a lot of fun because it allows you to play with elements of a character that you might ignore if you were dressing for a tropical climate. Like a lot of Disney's characters that are from the animal kingdom, Remy looks great using layers.

Let's start with the obvious—Remy is a rat, so this calls for a lot of gray. Begin by creating a monochromatic look using knits and jeans, and layer the look with a gray coat to keep you warm while you're out exploring the park.

The accessories are where you can start to add a little bit of color in the form of a pretty rose tone. These pink winter boots will keep your toes warm while helping you look stylish. You could opt for a low heel as well, or even a pale

pink sneaker—regardless, don't forget warm socks. Don't forget about your hands, either! Stay cozy in a pair of pink gloves. I also added a "spoon" ring for a special extra detail

The hat is my favorite part. There is no better way to re-create Remy's adorable ears in the colder months than with a knit beanie featuring double pom-poms. You'll be warm and comfy, for sure. Have fun at Disneyland Paris, and don't forget to make a reservation at Remy's restaurant, Bistrot Chez Rémy! Thanks to your *petite souris* style, you'll experience Remy's restaurant just as he intended you to!

Hong Kong Disneyland

It's not the biggest property in the world, and that's why I love it.

You can take in the whole park at your own pace. Don't let its size discourage you—there are many unique experiences at Hong Kong Disneyland that you cannot find anywhere else in the world.

The view down Main Street, U.S.A., is unlike any other. Behind the castle are miles of cascading jungle and mountains. Take a moment before venturing into the park to stand at the train station and absorb the view.

Hong Kong also has the best version of It's a Small World. Their ride features hidden Disney characters among the dolls in the regions that relate to their story. For instance, when you're driving through the British area, keep an eye out for Peter Pan and the Darlings flying around. Over in North America, you'll find Pocahontas overlooking a cliff with Flit and Meeko nearby.

There is no ride experience quite like Mystic Manor, which exists nowhere else in the world. It takes the place of the Haunted Mansion, but it has a completely different plot behind it. In fact, there aren't any ghosts at all! This ride is all about magic and a mischievous little monkey named Albert, who will steal your heart almost immediately. I won't give away spoilers; you'll have to see it for yourself!

If I were to encourage you to visit Hong Kong Disneyland at a particular time of year, it would be during Halloween. The Halloween decorations in Toy Story Land are incredible—they have all of Sid's creations on display, larger than life. And one Disney-bound that works year-round is Woody!

Woody

Woody is a great Disney-bound for those looking to keep it simple, but it might not seem that way when you're looking at him. Not every element of Woody's outfit needs to be used when creating a

Disney-bound for him. There are certain aspects of his look that really help to create his recognizable image, whereas other parts of his outfit are merely interchangeable accessories. I'll usually omit his cow-print vest and just add a cow-print detail somewhere else instead.

So let's start with a yellow plaid button-down shirt. It doesn't matter if the plaid is exactly like his—yellow plaid is yellow plaid! People will understand the vibe you're going for. It can get pretty hot and humid in Hong Kong, so trade his jeans for a pair of denim shorts instead. Do a French tuck to show off your belt!

Since the park is on the smaller side, I opted for a pair of brown boots that have a bit of a heel to them, but you can still get that cowboy boot vibe with

flat boots or sneakers! Protect yourself from the sun in style with a brown wide-brim fedora in lieu of a cowboy hat.

Though some climates may allow for a red bandanna tied around your neck, Hong Kong is not one of them. When high noon approaches, you won't want to have any items of clothing that you don't need. I traded in the bandanna for a bracelet that has the same paisley print on red fabric. A sheriff isn't complete without his star-shaped badge, so to finish off the look, I found a pair of sheriff's badge earrings that are perfect for enjoying a day of adventures at Hong Kong Disneyland!

Shanghai Disneyland

Shanghai Disneyland is Disney's NEWEST park!

Visiting this park is amazing because every ride features only the very latest in jaw-dropping technology. There are so many rides that are unlike any other rides you can find around the world—even if the themes are similar, the experience will be a unique one.

Thanks to this incredible new technology, their Pirates of the Caribbean ride is one of a kind—it takes you to the depths of the ocean. If you've ever gone snorkeling before, you'll know that feeling when you first submerge your face in the water and have to tell your brain that it's okay to breathe underwater. That's how realistic their Pirates of the Caribbean ride is!

One area of Shanghai Disneyland that is nothing if not an incredible Disney-bounding backdrop is the maze inspired by Tim Burton's *Alice in Wonderland*. Just about any Wonderland character would fit perfectly into this experience, but when you stumble across the Mad Hatter's Tea Party, you'll understand why I'm encouraging you to create a Disney-bound for the Mad Hatter himself!

The Mad Hatter

A very merry unbirthday to you! The Mad Hatter is quite the stylish gent, but when we start to block out his color scheme, it can get a little, well . . . mad! Depending on the image you're using as a reference, he comes in all shades of turquoise, teal, olive, and chartreuse! Due to this fact, you have a little flexibility with how you build out your Disney-bound. As long as you work in that general color palette, you can take it in any direction. Color isn't really the most important part of his outfit anyway—that would be his hat! You can dress him up, dress him down . . . keep him casual or get really crazy with him.

In the Disney-bounding community, there are a lot of Disney fans who also love vintage fashion—so let's take this look in that direction!

I've started by layering an olive button-down under a chartreuse blazer (with a teacup-shaped pin on the lapel). For the bottoms, let's play off that olive tone with a lighter shade of olive trousers. I believe that the Mad Hatter would have a little fun with his

socks, don't you? Adding a pair of wild argyle socks will give a little pop of personality—and the teal oxford shoes will give the appearance that we're not all mad here!

A vintage-inspired snap-brim fedora is a great take on his classic chapeau. Finish off the look with a turquoise bow tie just like the Mad Hatter's!

These elements are very specific to the dapper style that I chose for this Bound, but you never need to incorporate EVERY detail of a Disney character's design. For the Mad Hatter, the most important elements are his hat and an overall green color palette. The rest is really up to your interpretation.

Tokyo Disney Resort

Tokyo Disneyland and Tokyo DisneySea are as amazing as you imagine them to be! Japanese Disney fans have their own style, interests, character preferences, and community, so getting to witness it firsthand is quite the unique experience. That alone is enough of a reason for me to recommend going to this park.

If you're an *Aladdin* fan, you'll definitely want to check out Tokyo DisneySea. The Agrabah Marketplace area should be a land all on its own. Not only is it gigantic, but if you're a fan of the Genie, you will be able to find SO MUCH merchandise dedicated to this lovable blue character. The love for Aladdin and the Genie on display is its own tourist draw!

It's also at this park that you will find an unconditional love for Duffy the Disney Bear and his friends. For those not familiar with Duffy, he is Mickey Mouse's teddy bear, and he comes alive in Mickey's imagination! As the story goes, Minnie Mouse hand-sewed Duffy for Mickey Mouse and gifted it to him to keep him company during his long sea voyages. The phenomenal success of Duffy led to the creation of his friends: a crafty bear friend, ShellieMay; an artistic cat, Gelatoni; a hardworking dancer rabbit, StellaLou; an inventive foodie dog, CookieAnn; and a kindhearted musician turtle, 'Olu Mel. Their interactions are the basis of heartwarming "iyashi" (a Japanese word meaning comfort, healing, and the sense of being cared for) stories of friendship and collaboration.

Duffy the Disney Bear

Y ou can't go wrong with an adorable Disney-bound based on Duffy! You can find him at a few parks around the world, but it's safe to say that Tokyo Disneyland, Shanghai Disneyland, Hong Kong Disneyland, and Aulani have an extra-large space for Duffy in their hearts. His nautical style and cute personality are completely on trend with what Asian Disney fans love to wear. Let's keep it simple and stylish with a white sailor-inspired dress for this look.

Perhaps you don't want to sport a dress. There are plenty other fun nautical silhouettes that we can play with for this Duffy Disney-bound, like a sailor blouse, for instance. If you really wanted to take your Duffy Disney-bound on a more minimalistic route, a white T-shirt with a red scarf tied around your neck would be just fine. Duffy wears a cute little sailor hat, and you could really play up the vibe by adding a fisherman's cap to your look—but if a hat's not your style, you don't need it.

If you choose not to go in the dress direction, you have your choice of colors for bottoms. Technically, if you were to follow the rules of color blocking, Duffy's bottom half is the tan tone of his teddy bear fur. If you'd rather not wear that shade, you could also use the white bottoms of your choice for this look.

The tan shade carries through to the feet. I've included a pair of cute and comfy tan flats, but any pair of cute tan shoes works just as well! For his teddy bear accessories, I wanted to stick with something like what you can find at the Tokyo Disneyland stores, which is why I included an official Duffy bag.

Chapter 6

Taking Your Bound to the Next Level

At this point, it's safe to say you're a Disney-bounding pro!

We've talked about everything from color blocking to accessories to unique ways you can rock your Disney-bound around the world. But we're not quite done yet. There is still more ground to cover. Let's take your Disney-bound to the next level! When I say the next level, I don't mean ways to perfect your Bound. After all, any Disney-bound is perfect as long as you're comfortable and can express your personal style!

So what does it mean to take it to the next level? Well, who says that you have to Disney-bound as a single character? Why not Disney-bound as an entire film—pulling inspiration from multiple characters and using a particular backdrop in the film to set the tone? Or maybe you could Disney-bound as your favorite ride! The thing I love about Disney rides is the way they really immerse you in the theme. So why not design an outfit that's dripping in that theme, whatever it is? Or what about food? The Disney Parks are known for their iconic snacks, so why not use your Bound to declare your love for an iconic Disney Park treat? This is where you can really let your creativity loose and explore the magic of Disney through your own interpretation.

And keep in mind that you don't have to be at a Disney Park to rock that Disney-bound. There are so many places and events in your life where you can incorporate a Bound. Consider Disney-bounding at the next wedding you attend, if it suits the mood—or even Disney-bounding at your own wedding!

Disney-Bounding in Groups

Just like life, Disney-bounding is better with friends! I prefer Disney-bounding in a group. It's so much fun to see all your friends come together, looking and feeling their very best. It's also a great way to explore your friends' personal styles. You can see how they interpret a character in a different way than you do!

There are many creative ways that you can Disney-bound in groups:

By Category

Perhaps you can each select a Disney Princess, or maybe the Disney villains are more your speed. Bounding a Disney category will allow each one of your friends to choose a Disney character who really resonates with them and their personal style.

By Film

This is a great option when you have a large group of friends who would all like to Disney-bound. Challenge yourselves to see if you can Bound the full cast of characters!

In Small Groups

Sometimes it can be very complicated to organize a large group of people. Don't stress! Encourage your large group to split off into smaller ones. Maybe three of you could be the *Aristocats* kittens, and another duo could be the Genie and the Magic Carpet. You don't all have to share the same theme to have a great day of Disney-bounding.

Free-for-All

Your group doesn't have to match. Sometimes it's just fun to spend the day together. One of your friends may have all the items to make a perfect Rocket Raccoon, but you want to Bound as Snow White. You can still get a big group together and have the best Disney-bounding day ever!

My only tip when it comes to organizing a group Disney-bound is to make sure you have fun with it. It won't be fun if YOU'RE not having fun! Let's say you're organizing a group Disney-bound and you have two folks who want to be Belle. That's no problem! There can definitely be two Belles if that really means a lot to both Bounders. Perhaps one can wear a Disney-bound for Belle's blue dress while the other wears Belle's yellow dress! You can even have two Belles in yellow dresses, because each person's interpretation of a character has its own twist.

What I love about getting my friends together for a Disney-bound at a Disney Park is the way it changes up how we experience the park that day. Our characters could inspire us to dine at a restaurant we don't usually go to, or find a new backdrop for a perfect group photo. Disney-bounding usually takes us on a different path than we'd travel otherwise, and you might find it does this for you and your friends, too!

With all the creativity and effort that goes into creating the perfect group Disney-bound, you'll want to make sure you capture the moment in a photo so you always have that fun day to look back on. Try to think of a spot, or maybe even a few, that matches the theme of your Disney-bounds. Maybe there are also meet and greets available for some characters you'd like to visit in your Disney-bound!

Disney-Bounding a Film

When you Disney-bound an entire film, your outfit strays from a more precise interpretation of a Disney character and starts to become more of an immersive abstract interpretation instead. The story you tell with your outfit won't just be that of one character. It will involve a wide array of characters and story lines, telling the entire plot through the accessories you wear. Your clothing may be a mash-up of multiple characters' color palettes, silhouettes, or styles. It could also be a backdrop, using your accessories as a way to incorporate multiple characters into one outfit. You have the opportunity to get really creative with this one—let your imagination run wild!

Toy Story

Let's create a Disney-bound for the Pixar film *Toy Story* so you can see how it's done. This film is a great one to Disney-bound since it contains so many unique characters. It also has one very iconic setting that many recognize, and that's Andy's room! We'll use it as the base for this Disney-bound.

To set the tone of this Disney-bound, I've found the perfect blue sky/white cloud skater dress. Andy's iconic wallpaper will be recognizable to others, and as they notice your accessories, they will begin to understand that there is a theme to your look! I've layered this outfit with a light blue denim jacket because we'll want to use some Disney enamel pins as character inspiration later on.

Let's start adding a few characters to this outfit! Cowboy boots are a cute way to give a nod to Woody. You can take your Woody inspiration to the next level by using permanent marker to write "ANDY" on the bottom of one of your shoes. It won't be visible to most people, but you'll know it's there! I think that's kind of fun! Bo Peep is represented too, using a Bo Peep–inspired mini backpack.

The Aliens from *Toy Story* are

another fan fav, so I've used a necklace that features one of the little green men. You could also find one with the infamous Claw—oooOOOooo! (You just read that in their voice, didn't you?)

Rex is one of my top *Toy Story* characters because I relate to a character who is in a constant state of panic. I've represented him in this Disney-bound with a Tyrannosaurus rex ring!

Last but not least, let's add a few enamel pins! I of course included Buzz Lightyear, Jessie, and Bullseye!

How I've interpreted a *Toy Story* Disney-bound is different from how you might design one. You can use my suggestions as a guide or feel free to completely break the mold and design something entirely different!

Disney-Bounding Food

When the *DisneyBound* blog really took off, I started to receive follower requests for Bounds of all sorts of Disney-related experiences. Not only did they want to see characters and parks, they were looking for inspiration to Disney-bound food! From pineapple soft serve to Mickey Premium Ice Cream Bars, the requests were coming in. I'll never forget the message I opened up that read, "I know this is weird . . . but can you make a Disney-bound for a turkey leg?"

Disney foodies can take their Bounds in a variety of directions. You can Disney-bound the food itself, or perhaps it's the vibe of the restaurant where the item is sold that's more fitting for your personal style!

Disney-Bounding a Ride

Similar to Disney-bounding a film, you can Disney-bound an entire ride! It's a special way to pay homage to the level of creativity that went into these rides.

There are a few ways you can do it—especially as everyone interprets these experiences differently, and the same ride may resonate differently with people. Perhaps, for you, a ride is represented by the cast members who greet you at the entrance. Each attraction (or land) comes with a unique costume that its hosts get to wear. Disney-bounding this costume is one way to Bound a ride.

Another way is by Disney-bounding as the entire ride itself, just like how we Disney-bounded an entire film. Selecting an iconic backdrop or fashion trends unique to that ride will be your foundation. You can use accessories to incorporate different characters, situations you encounter on the ride, or even quotes from the ride itself!

You could also select your favorite character on that ride. Perhaps your favorite is Redd from Pirates of the Caribbean or Figment from Journey Into Imagination. Characters we meet on rides may not be featured in any movies, but to Disney Parks aficionados, they're as famous and beloved as anyone else in the official Disney character rolodex!

Pineapple Soft Serve

The most iconic (and attractive) Disney food is the pineapple soft serve. This is a frozen pineapple treat that can be found in the Adventureland area of most Disney Parks. Visually, it's a swirl of white and yellow; you can get the soft serve by itself, or enjoy a pineapple float topped with pineapple soft serve. Sometimes it will come garnished with a cherry and a little paper umbrella. It's truly the perfect tropical treat for a hot day at the Disney Parks!

What I find the most fun about Disney-bounding a food item is that, to an even greater extent than other Bounds, there really isn't a right or wrong way to do it. It's entirely up to you and how you interpret the food item—and how you've had it served to you in the past. Since you'll most likely be sporting this Disney-bound at a Disney Park, let's make it an easy and fun one to wear! To keep it light, let's start with a light yellow playsuit to represent the pineapple juice in the float. The drink tends to be a darker shade of yellow on the bottom and a lighter cream shade on top—so let's play with that color gradient in this Bound. For the shoes, I've used those yellow sneakers that I promised you we'd be using a

lot. For the cream on top, let's use a cream-colored hair wrap. The tie on top reminds me of the little swirl of pineapple soft serve!

As the pineapple flavor is the most important element of the pineapple soft serve, let's go into our collection of kitschy bags and use a pineapple-shaped bag. Suddenly, what was just a yellow outfit begins to take the shape of

a pineapple soft serve! I've also included a pair of pineapple-shaped earrings.

When making a Disney-bound for a Disney food item, there isn't always a lot to pull from, so make sure you are playing with all the available elements.

Now for the cherry on top, literally! To complete this Disney-bound, I've included a maraschino cherry ring.

Haunted Mansion
The Ride

Is there anything more iconic about the Haunted Mansion than that ornate Victorian-inspired black-and-purple wallpaper that can be found throughout all its hallways? Let's use this wallpaper as our foundation for this Haunted Mansion Disney-bound!

I'd like to take it in a vintage direction. Instead of finding an item of clothing with that exact print, let's use a

black-and-purple lace dress that evokes it without being too literal. And, as many of the ghosts we meet throughout the ride are dressed in Victorian fashion, let's use that as inspiration for the rest of our outfit. I've paired the dress with a pair of black lace-up ankle boots because they are spooky and modern, yet pay tribute to the shoe trends of the Victorian era.

If you've had the opportunity to ride the Haunted Mansion, you'll know that you experience this foreboding household on a Doom Buggy, which reminds me quite a bit of a coffin. As death is sort of the main theme on this ride, I think we should really play with that in the accessories we select. This black coffin handbag reminds me of the Doom Buggy and helps point to the general theme of this outfit.

At one point on the ride, we meet Madame Leota, a fortune-teller trapped in a crystal ball. She helps conjure up the gleeful ghosts who dwell in this residence. I've represented her with a crystal ball ring! For the necklace, I chose a rather morbid pedant in the shape of an ax. We learn in the attic that this is Constance Hatchaway's weapon of choice, as sadly each one of her husbands seems to wind up missing his head.

There are 999 playful specters who reside inside the Haunted Mansion, so it's impossible to make sure each one is portrayed in your Disney-bound. However, little ghost stud earrings are representative of all who roam the halls of this residence!

Haunted Mansion

The Tightrope Walker

Instead of Disney-bounding an entire ride, you can also select a character unique to the ride. The Haunted Mansion has a lot of distinctive characters we meet as we journey through the halls of the home, such as the Hatbox

Ghost, Constance Hatchaway, and the Hitchhiking Ghosts. But some of the most iconic faces from the Haunted Mansion are not even ghosts. "Is this room actually stretching?" The stretching portraits in the first room we enter as we make our way to the Doom Buggies feature four characters all slowly unveiling a sinister secret as the exitless room stretches to the sky.

Let's create a Disney-bound for the tightrope walker, as she seems to be a community favorite included by many on their "must Bound" lists. Remember, you don't have to re-create her outfit exactly. It's more about matching the vibe. For this look, let's start by using a purple camisole with a short-sleeved purple cardigan on top. You can choose to do up one button on your cardigan to match the silhouette of her collar.

Rather than try to find a skirt that looks just like hers, let's keep it a bit more vague. Since it features a green floral pattern on a white fabric, I've pulled a white skirt with a pink-and-green floral print. Remember, your personal style leaves the design of this Disney-bound completely open to your own interpretation! This tightrope walker wouldn't be complete without her ballet slippers, which we can re-create with a pair of pink flats. I've also added a necklace with an umbrella charm—it's much easier than carrying a parasol around all day!

I think that what makes her portrait the most memorable of them all is the contrast between her soft femininity in the form of ballet slippers and a purple color palette . . . and the tough green alligator waiting beneath her. Let's make that contrast pop in the outfit we design by completing the Bound with an alligator-shaped handbag!

Haunted Mansion

The Ride Attendant

Some rides give their cast members very unique costumes to wear to really immerse the riders in the journey they are experiencing. The Haunted Mansion is one of those rides. The attendants' forest-green butler and maid uniforms make you feel like you are being greeted by the mansion's only living caretakers. Disney-bounding as these attendants is another way that you can pay homage to your favorite ride through fashion!

It's important to note that this Disney-bound should *not* be an exact duplicate of their uniform if you plan on wearing it to the Disney Parks. Your outfit may have a similar vibe and overall tone, but for the safety of the cast members and guests, it's important to make sure that you won't actually be confused for one of the hosts. On that note, while the cast members wear name tags as part of their uniforms, you do not need this detail in your Disney-bound. You are a guest, after all!

You could create a look for the maid's striped forest-green uniform. The obvious place to start is with a green-striped button-down short-sleeve top. Then just add a pair of forest-green shorts and a pair of black shoes that you feel comfortable wearing for a day at the Disney Parks! Instead of a white lace maid's hairpiece, use a black or white hair wrap. You'll want something to carry your things in, so perhaps you could complete this look with a coffin-shaped backpack! Have fun in your Haunted Mansion Disney-bound . . . whatever direction you choose to take it in.

Disney-Bounding
Prom

They say that prom is supposed to be one of the best nights of your life! Why not have a little extra fun with your prom-dress shopping by looking for the perfect gown to match the style of one of your most-loved Disney characters? Disney-bounding for your prom can be a lot of fun because the options for bright and colorful gowns are endless! This is your moment to find a gown that expresses exactly who you are. Many Disney-bounders find that subtly dressing as their favorite Disney characters helps them embody the characters and all they represent. Perhaps it's when you're Disney-bounding as Tiana from *The Princess and the Frog* that you'll feel your most confident. What Disney character do you want to represent you at prom?

Prom is a fun event to Disney-bound to because the clothing can be SO colorful. You really have almost every color palette at your fingertips. Start off by choosing what Disney character you'd like to channel and then pick a gown that matches their primary color. For instance, if you're thinking of Disney-bounding Vanellope von Schweetz for your prom, you could choose a turquoise gown. Then have fun with a lot of candy-inspired accessories to symbolize her life in *Sugar Rush*! Or maybe you're looking for a way to add some Disney inspiration to your prom tux? Someone like Prince Eric translates really well to a suit. Start off with a navy blue jacket and pants, and pair them with a white dress shirt and black shoes. You can accessorize this look with a red belt and a nautical tie inspired by this sea-loving prince. Turn the page to see the Jasmine-inspired prom Disney-bound I created just for this book!

RunDisney

A RunDisney race is unlike any other half marathon. Regardless of whether you enjoy running, a RunDisney race might be just the right event to get you in the mood. There is something about that extra touch of Disney magic that helps carry you across the finish line! The first 5K I ever ran was with RunDisney—before then, I tried to avoid running of any kind. That 5K run turned into a 10K run, and before I knew it, I was running half marathons on both coasts at Disneyland and Walt Disney World.

A RunDisney race weekend usually inlcudes multiple races: a 5K, a 10K, and a half marathon. Sometimes there will even be a full marathon. When you arrive at Walt Disney World or Disneyland, there is a special energy in the air.

On your marks, get set, GO! Since so many unique Disney characters will greet you along the race course, you'll definitely want to stop for a few photos along the way. So make sure that whatever outfit you create for your race has a safe pocket for your phone so you don't miss those amazing photo ops!

No Disney group loves to play dress-up more than RunDisney racers. You'll see some AMAZING costumes during your race that will leave you wondering, "How are they running in that?!" If running in a costume isn't for you, this is where Disney-bounding comes into play. When it comes to athletic wear, you'll have a lot of clothing categories and accessories to play with!

The first RunDisney half marathon I ran was Marvel themed. I wanted to choose a Disney-bound that would be easy to color-block, using athletic wear that also reminded me, "You can do this!" I couldn't think of a more fitting character than the Incredible Hulk. He is a really simple one to re-create as he is green on top, purple or blue in the middle, and green on the bottom!

Another great character for a to Bound for RunDisney is Snow White—see how I interpreted a look for her on page 130.

Jasmine

Princess Jasmine is such a great role model. Her "I am not a prize to be won" attitude will have you confidently waltzing into that prom knowing that you ARE a princess tonight!

When you're prom shopping, it's okay if you can't find a prom dress that's the perfect shade of Princess Jasmine turquoise. Any shade of teal or greenish-blue will be a great place to start building this Bound! If it suits your personal style, you could even sport a two-piece prom dress to pay homage to the silhouette of Princess Jasmine's outfit! It would definitely be a different vibe from what a lot of other girls wear and help your dress stand out.

For her shoes, I recommend comfort over fashion, especially if you aren't used to wearing heels. Heels can be very uncomfortable—women often find the

brand or style that works for them and then stick with it, and if you're not sure you've found yours yet, you'll want to be careful. Make sure the shoes you pick don't have any painful points when you put them on. Any uncomfortable rubbing when you try them on in the store will manifest into painful blisters within hours once you start walking around in

them. For a prom Bound, I like to give Jasmine gold shoes. These will be easy to find in just about any shoe store with a formal selection.

Let's talk accessories! Jasmine has a lot of beautiful gold accessories, so have fun with your choices. I've selected a pair of gold teardrop earrings, similar to hers, along with a teal cocktail ring that reminds me of the jewel on her headband. Since this is a prom look, you can really have fun with the hair

accessories. I was able to find a gold headband that kind of reminds me of the one Princess Jasmine wears!

You can really have fun with your prom clutch! It's your one chance to really go all out and shine the way you want to. Search the Internet for really unique clutches to complement your prom dress. I selected a bedazzled tiger-shaped clutch so that Princess Jasmine is not without a Rajah by her side!

Snow White

I can't write a book on Disney-bounding without talking about one of the most recognizable Disney characters. She's the very first princess in the collection of Disney films, so I try to pay homage to her whenever possible. It's thanks to her success that Disney is what it is today! Snow White is really fun and easy to Disney-bound, as the most important aspect of her outfit is the color blocking. Similar to Anna, it's easy to create a look for her with just a few items of clothing. As long as your top half is mainly blue with red accents and your bottom half is yellow—who you're Disney-bounding will be very obvious to the Disney-bounding community!

How does she translate into race wear? Let's take a look! For her top half, we want to focus on blue but include a pop of red. I decided to use a blue athletic top that has some unique cutouts so a red sports bra will show through. The bottom half is really easy; you just need a simple pair of yellow running shorts! In lieu of a hair bow, why not use a red sweatband to keep hair

and sweat out of your eyes on your big race day?

For a racing outfit, matching your shoes to your Disney-bound is much less important. You want to make sure you're comfortable while you're out on that racecourse. The shoes you've trained in are the ones you should run in that day. If they match your character, that's a bonus, but make sure you're putting your comfort and safety first! Rather than carry an apple with you during your big race, you can find a different way to represent it. Shoelace clips are one fun way you can do this. These clips string onto your laces and can help you carry Snow White's most iconic piece with you wherever you go!

Chapter 7

The Community

I want to take a moment and introduce you to just SOME of the members that make up the large community of Disney-bounders around the world.

Disney-bounding would not be what it is today without the people who love to do it. I often say that if it weren't for the Disney-bounders who joyously express their love for their favorite characters through fashion, I would just be a girl with a Disney fashion blog. It's Disney-bounders who truly give this movement wings!

There are thousands of Disney-bounders around the world. They come from different walks of life, they've lived different life experiences and speak different languages . . . but one thing they have in common is their love for Disney, and they love to find ways to create magic in their everyday lives.

Check out #DISNEYBOUND, #DISNEYBOUNDER, and #DISNEYBOUNDING on popular social media platforms to find more Bounders like those featured in this book!

"My husband and I love to Disney-bound together! We enjoy using vintage clothing to express our Disney style. Disney-bounding allows us to be creative, and we love to take on the challenge of obscure characters, like this look inspired by Zed and Addison from the Disney Channel Original Movie *Z-O-M-B-I-E-S*!"
—Cailey

"Disney-bounding is a way for me to show my love for Disney. Disney characters often recognize or try to guess who my Disney-bound character is. The reactions I get from them are simply magical!"
—Kana

"This was the first time many of us had been to Galaxy's Edge, so as huge *Star Wars* fans, we couldn't *not* Disney-bound. It really helps you feel like part of the magical world around you."
—Anna

"Disney-bounding has been a great way for us to express ourselves creatively as a couple. We love being able to work together to create outfits that showcase our shared loved of all things Disney. Through the act of Disney-bounding, we've been fortunate enough to form meaningful friendships with like-minded people in a community we're all passionate about. We have fun and we look good doing it!"
—Lizzy and James

"There are so many characters in the Disney universe to love and connect with, and I love how creative the Disney-bounding community is. You can make Disney-bounding your own, whether you want to do a full-out elegant Bound of a princess or a casual hint of polka dots on your everyday outfit to represent Minnie. I decided to Disney-bound as Marie from *The Aristocats* because she is such a sassy, feminine feline! I have an absolute love for all things pink and white and Marie is definitely very ladylike, just like me!"
—Karen

"Our favorite part about Disney-bounding is getting to celebrate both the iconic and lesser-known Disney characters that influenced our childhoods so much! Some of our favorite more obscure characters are Bonnie's colorful cast of toys introduced in *Toy Story 3*—Buttercup, Mr. Pricklepants, and Trixie! We loved both their unique personalities and fun designs, so it made for an exciting challenge to bring them to life in our Disney-bounds!"
—Kelsey, April, and Yvette

"I love Disney-bounding because it's a way for me to express my creativity and passion for both Disney and fashion. My favorite thing about it is that I get to find new ways to style pieces that I already have in my closet over and over again! The Disney-bound community has also connected me with so many amazing people who share similar interests, and some have even become my closest friends in real life!"
—Keshia

"From day one, I have been a true Disney kid. From having a luau-themed *Lilo & Stitch* birthday party to visiting the parks each year as our family summer vacation, I was obsessed. However, my true love for Disney and more importantly Disneyland didn't bloom until the beginning of 2017. I had just moved back to California to begin my graduate teaching credential program, and I was scared out of my wits. I was living on my own for the very first time, and my closest friends had moved out of the area due to starting their careers and 'growing up,' so it felt a lot like starting over. But then, one day, I was aimlessly scrolling through Instagram and discovered so many people who were going to the parks and doing these incredible photo shoots inspired by beloved characters, and my mind was blown! These people were truly making magic and bringing a whole new meaning to park days, and I wanted in. Little did I know that digging through the thrift store finds in my closet to create some Bounds and reaching out to strangers on the Internet would bring me so much joy. Through Disney-bounding, I have gained so much confidence in myself and learned to accept that I am beautiful despite society's standards. I can express my creativity through my love for fashion and my favorite Disney characters, all while educating others about dwarfism and making a few friends along the way."
—Rachel

"Disney-bounding helped me find a home and community when I moved to Los Angeles, and has become my creative outlet. I love searching online for unique items for future Disney-bounds as well as making my own accessories and designs. Purses are my favorite way to accessorize a Disney-bound since they are functional and stylish at the same time! Disney-bounding, and the friends I've made through it, has made my life, as well as every trip to Disneyland, unique and magical!"
—Anne

"After years of trying to perfect my own style and reflect self-expression through every outfit, I noticed I am able to do that most genuinely through Disney-bounding. Disney-bounding has become my life. For every piece I purchase, in the back of my mind I'm saying, 'I've got a character for that.' I came across the Disney-bound community in a time in my life where I needed something to look forward to and something to help me feel comfortable in my own skin. At first it was me hiding behind a character, but with growth and the support from fellow Disney-bounders, it became me showing the world Dom as any character. This community has been so open, inspiring, and comforting. What most would call strangers on the Internet I now call friends who have helped me discover and witness some of the best parts of me."

—Dom

"In 2015, Disney-bounding was brought to my attention, and I immediately started putting outfits together, styling them to look similar to Disney characters, and matching them to my hair bows and mouse ears!

"Later that fall, my boyfriend and I went to Dapper Day, Disney-bounding as Lilo and Stitch, and our outfits were such a hit that we were getting stopped every couple of steps because everyone wanted their picture taken with us! I think that was one of the most life-changing days of my life. Not only was my dress, which I handmade from scratch, getting a lot of attention, but that was the same day I got engaged . . . while Disney-bounding! Four years later, I still Disney-bound whenever I go to the parks, or whenever I go to see a new Disney movie. I was inspired by Buzz Lightyear and put this outfit together in honor of the *Toy Story 4* release in theaters!"

—Stephanie

"As a plus-sized woman, I spent a great deal of my life hiding from my body. Though I loved fashion, I couldn't help feeling that the industry just wasn't made for someone who looked like me. It wasn't until I realized that I had the power to decide for myself that I started to abandon the rules I had been taught. I spent my childhood immersed in the magic of Disney and fairy tales, always wanting to grow up to be a princess. Disney-bounding provided an outlet for me to express that, allowing me to 'leave my tower' to become my own kind of princess."
—Heather

"*Mary Poppins* is our favorite Disney movie, and we even had a *Mary Poppins*-themed wedding! We love Disney-bounding because we get to express our love for the movies in our own unique fashion style. It's also fun because each person's outfit has its own characteristics, and there are no right or wrong answers."
—Katsu

"I chose to do a Judy Hopps Disney-bound with a little bit of a vintage twist. The sweater is circa 1970 and my pants are from Unique Vintage. The thing I love most about Disney-bounding is bringing my own style to each of the characters I Disney-bound, and I love to see how others in the community do the same. I love being part of this community with so many creative people and all the love and support everyone I have met in this community has for each other!"
—Malerie

"With Disney-bounding, the goal is to create an outfit that you could wear out and about every day."

"The Disney-bound community has created a welcoming place for anyone, no matter the age, race, size, or background, to have the freedom to transform into our favorite Disney characters! Through Disney-bounding, I've found the sky's the limit on fusing my personal style with a little imagination to become anything (and anyone) I've always dreamed of being . . . even a princess with glowing hair, chameleons, and frying pans as accessories! I'm thankful for this amazing community and all that it represents!"

—Jenn

"*The Little Mermaid* is one of my favorite movies, the 'Kiss the Girl' dress is my favorite outfit that Ariel wears, and that's why I chose it. While envisioning and then executing Disney-inspired outfits is fun in and of itself, being able to share my creations with an enthusiastic community of like-minded people makes it so much better! And seeing everyone else's ideas, creativity, and positivity is amazing! Joining and being a part of this community from the beginning when it was only about three hundred people to what it is now is beyond anything I could've imagined."

—Christina

"I am Disney-bounding as Doctor Strange! I love to Disney-bound because no one is left behind. Everyone has a chance to showcase their passion for Disney magic no matter their color, size, or shape. Being a part of this diverse group makes going to the parks even better!"

—Pernell

"What makes Disney-bounding so special is that it lets you share your passion for your favorite Disney characters, while being free to be completely yourself."

— Colette, Tiffany, Briana, Christina, and Audrey

"Disney-bounding is my creative way of exercising my love of a character. I feel that each character has a distinctive personality all his/her own, and style is such a fun avenue to showcase not only the character's personality, but my own. I see myself in so many of the characters that Disney has created, and Disney-bounding gives that vision a voice that people can see."

— Ranitra

"Ever since I was little, I've always enjoyed dressing up like my favorite characters. Disney-bounding has given me the opportunity to continue that love as an adult. My best friend, Bryan, introduced me to Disney-bounding the first time we hung out, and it's a tradition that we do it every time we visit Disneyland or travel. I've also made many new friends through Disney-bounding and enjoy the support in the community to just express yourself freely."

— Kelly

"I'm a huge Disney fan, and Disney-bounding has always been my favorite part of heading to Disneyland. The cultural norms for straight men say I shouldn't dress up or wear certain colors. With Disney-bounding, I've broken out of that and left my comfort zone to try new styles, to be a little extra, to be bold, and to just have fun with myself and not take life too seriously. Says a lot about Disney-bounding when you can find yourself in dressing up like someone else."

— Bryan

"When I became a young mom, I found myself at home a lot, out of the workforce, and feeling distant from the person I used to be. So I started tapping into my creative side again. When a friend introduced me to Disney-bounding, it quickly became one of my favorite creative outlets. Mixing up your wardrobe, finding pieces that reflect Disney characters without being literal, pairing items you wouldn't have considered pairing before, reusing the same clothes and accessories for different looks, pulling an outfit together with a perfect accessory . . . this is all very creative. It's been over six years since I first began Disney-bounding, and it's still one of my very favorite creative outlets."

—Chelsea

"From just looking at my closet, I was able to put together a Disney-bound of Winnie the Pooh. And that's how easy it is to Disney-bound! You don't have to go and buy a whole new outfit to participate. You can just work with the things you already have. For me, Disney-bounding really helped me come out of my shell. I was shy, and really nervous to step out of my comfort zone, especially when it came to new clothing styles. Once I started to Disney-bound, I was able to really express myself through fashion and my love of Disney."

—Maryssa

"Disney-bounding has allowed me to feel comfortable, happy, and beautiful in a way that nothing else ever has. Emulating my favorite characters through fashion isn't just fun—it's empowering. Abi and I gravitate toward determined, passionate characters that have strong bonds with one another. We chose WALL·E and EVE because we see ourselves in the care and kindness they show each other, and in the heartfelt way they fight for positive change in society."

—April

"I love Disney-bounding because I've always loved expressing myself through fashion, especially through vintage fashion, which is how I dress on a normal basis. Disney-bounding gave me the confidence to dress in vintage attire in my everyday life. I love making my own accessories and even adding small details to clothes to make them more recognizable as a character. I picked Bo Peep's new outfit in *Toy Story 4* because she's not portrayed as a damsel in distress. She's strong and independent while still being super cute, which is very much my own personality."
—Alyssa

"I love Disney-bounding because it gives me the opportunity to tap into my creative side while having a lot of fun putting together outfits that represent different Disney characters. It's even more enjoyable when someone recognizes my Disney-bound character. It has really built such a fun and interactive community to be a part of."
—Kirsten

"Our love for Disney-bounding started as a way to express our love for Disney through fashion. But over the years it has grown into so much more than that. We met each other as well as many of our closest friends because of our shared interest in Bounding, and we will be forever grateful for these amazing people who have come into our lives. Disney-bounding isn't just a trend; it's a community, and we love being a part of it."
—Erika and Alyssa

**D**isney-bounding is so much more than just replicating the costumes of Disney characters with your own wardrobe.

It's about expressing your self-confidence—or maybe even discovering it for the first time. When I first started blogging about Disney-bounding, I didn't think much about it other than how fun it was to create these outfits. It was a few months into the blog that I really began to learn what it means to others.

I started receiving messages from Disney-bounders who had not only discovered the fun of Disney-bounding, but had, through their experience, discovered and opened up new parts of themselves that they hadn't known existed or were struggling to find. Perhaps they'd never related to the celebrities in the fashion magazines, but thinking things like "What would Rapunzel wear if she were heading out today?" allowed them to discover a confidence that they didn't know existed.

One story in particular that has always stuck with me is the story of a Disney-bounder named April Barbossa. She included the story in a post she shared of herself Disney-bounding as Cinderella. What looked at first glance like nothing more than a girl dressing as one of her favorite Disney Princesses was actually a girl experiencing positivity for the first time in a long time. She wrote of her struggles with mental illness and an eating disorder that had left her feeling less than confident in who she was. It took a lot for her to even go out in public that day, but by putting on her Cinderella Disney-bound, she was able to not be April that day . . . she was able to be Cinderella. She was able to be beautiful and brave—a member of the Disney royal family. As the day went on, she realized that all the confidence and the beauty, both inside and out . . . these were not only Cinderella's qualities, they were her very own. While Bounding as Cinderella may have helped bring those qualities out in her, at the end of the day, when she took off her Disney-bound, she was able to recognize that it was April who had that amazing day, and there could be many more just like it in her future.

There are many other stories out there just like April's, and that's the true magic of Disney-bounding. It's kind of a hidden secret—not everyone knows that this magic exists. Many just see brightly colored clothes and a way to play dress-up as an adult . . . but it's so much more than that. On their lowest of days, Disney-bounding has helped people realize that they can actually trust themselves and who they truly are. That who they are is perfectly fine, because they, too, are royalty . . . they are warriors . . . they are everything they want to be and more.

There are many people in the world who love to tell us that we shouldn't be confident—that we shouldn't be happy with who we are. If someone insists on sharing a negative opinion about you, just know that is a reflection of who *they* are, and *not* who you are. I know it's one thing to hear this, but it's another thing to truly believe it. But the reality is, happy people, confident people—they don't go around trying to tear other people down. They don't speak their negative opinions into the universe in the hope that they might hurt someone else's feelings. Their negative opinions are just opinions, not facts.

Here's how Disney-bounding can help you restore your confidence. Instead of being affected by someone else's opinion of you, take that power away from people who don't deserve to have it . . . and give it to Snow White, give it to Ariel, give it to Minnie Mouse. They will lift you up and make you feel magical.

When you put on your Disney-bound, you embody that character. You take on their power, their sense of adventure, their growth. It's often said that self-confidence is the best outfit you can wear, and I think Disney-bounding really reflects that. Maybe there's something you would've never thought to wear, but that Cruella De Vil would . . . and for that reason, you discover that you CAN in fact pull it off.

It was through Disney-bounding Moana and thinking of the lesson she teaches us in her film that I realized what an important role self-confidence plays in her story. Moana teaches us that we do not need anyone's permission to be ourselves. I thought about it a lot that day and really walked away with a new sense of mental strength and confidence. Be proud of who you are. Take into consideration how far you've come and how much you've grown.

Your mind is very powerful, which is why we have to be careful of the conversations we have with ourselves. If we tell ourselves, "I can't wear that," or "That won't look good on me," we are doing nothing but lying to ourselves, which hurts us more than we know. Try to find a way to have more compassionate conversations with yourself. This can be easier said than done when you're in a place where you're doubting your potential to shine. So put on a Disney-bound for a character who inspires you. Allow that Disney character to live vicariously through you, and they will gift you with the lessons they've learned along the way. It's like the Disney character did all the hard work, and you just get to reap the benefits of strength, compassion, and confidence.

Be kind to yourself. You are just like any other Disney character. Mulan didn't start off her story as a warrior. *The Princess and the Frog* didn't kick off with the opening of Tiana's restaurant. Each Disney movie takes us on a journey of growth. The characters may stumble, they may make mistakes . . . they may doubt who they are or let others lead them astray. But it always turns out the way it's supposed to in the end. Believe in the universe. If you're feeling less than confident or you're not sure where you're headed in life . . . remember that you are on a journey, just like your Disney favorites. Trust your journey . . . it's usually the most interesting part of the film, don't you think?

I hope you find your authentic self through Disney-bounding. I hope it shows you that you have the power to be whoever you want to be—that you can be a princess whose gown was made by three comical fairies; you can be a lovable blue alien who crash-landed in Hawaii; or you can even be a big blue genie who grants your friends three wishes. But at the end of the day, when you take that Disney-bound off, I hope you realize that who you really want to be . . . who you're really *proud* to be . . . is yourself. You bring a touch of Disney magic to this world unlike any other.

Chapter
8

The Disney-Bounding Inauguration

It's time to make it official!

I've given you all the Disney-bounding tips and tricks, and now you can start on your own Disney-bounding adventure! But before you begin your new journey as a Disney-bounder, I want you to remember these important points:

Expressing your personal style is the most important things about Disney-bounding. Don't forget that there is no one quite like you, so make sure to show yourself off!

Always start with what's in your closet when building out a Disney-bound. You never know what Disney characters are hiding in there!

Yellow shoes are your new best friend!

A pair of brown ankle boots will go a long way.

If you are going to a Disney Park, refer to the rules on costuming before leaving your home or hotel for the day. It's essential to respect these rules when getting dressed in order to avoid disappointment at the gate of the park.

You don't need to be at a Disney Park to Disney-bound. It's a great way to find that touch of Disney magic wherever you are in the world.

Bags will help take your Disney-bound to that next level!

Keep an eye out for colored denim pants on sale! They will come in handy for creating quick and easy Disney-bounds!

It's important that the official characters at the Disney Parks are the only characters. Please do not pretend to be a character while you're at a Disney Park. If a guest or their child mistakes you for a character, correct them and let them know that you are a guest as well.

Disney-bounding is about expressing your love for your favorite character—not about looking exactly like them. Don't worry if your outfit may be less recognizable than others'. Everyone's style is different!

There are a lot of creative ways to incorporate items like props and capes into your outfit without actually having to use those items. Let your creativity soar!

The Disney-bound community is a global group of Disney-loving people who all express their creativity in different ways, and that's the most beautiful part about it. Be a flower that blossoms in your own way, and allow others to blossom in their own ways, too.

If you're having a tough time emotionally, lean on a Disney character to lift up your spirits. Disney-bounding as that character will not only help you pull style inspiration from them, but emotional support as well.

There is only one real rule of Disney-bounding, and it's that you always spread positivity wherever you are. Whether you're Disney-bounding or not, make sure you are a positive light in this world. If you see someone who looks fabulous, tell them. Give them a compliment. If you're at a Disney Park and you notice someone is Disney-bounding, let them know you love their outfit. You never know what people are dealing with on the inside. Passing along a compliment might just brighten someone's day.

And now, you're ready! You're officially a Disney-bounder. I'm so excited for you! You're about to make some fabulous Disney-bounds, meet a lot of amazing people, and discover that Disney magic can be found anywhere you are. All it takes is a little faith, trust, and pixie dust!

Acknowledgments

There are many people who deserve a portion of the credit for making this book happen. Much like a child, it took a village to raise Disney-bounding up to where it is today, and it wouldn't be what it is without their mental, emotional, and physical support. I would like to extend my greatest thanks to . . .

Gary Buchanan for giving me my first opportunity with The Walt Disney Company. If it weren't for your initial endorsement, *DisneyBound* might not have had any of the opportunities that came its way.

The Disney-bounding community for making Disney-bounding what it is today. If it weren't for your creative contributions to this fashion trend, Disney-bounding would not be at the scale that it is today. It's impossible to take complete credit for a movement that has been built up by so many creative people around the world.

Erin Zimring and her team for allowing me to fulfill a childhood dream by giving me the opportunity to write a book. It's a bucket list item that I'm still pinching myself over.

My parents for exposing me to the magic of Disney throughout my childhood.

Alisa, Alyssa, April, Audrey, Brandon, Briana, Colette, Dan, Erika, Garrett, James, Jessica, John, Kelsey, Leo, Lizzy, Sarah, Tiffany, Timmy, and Vince for always being down to be a bunch of adults who will play dress-up with me at any moment. I'm happy to have found my Neverland in our friendships!

Joschka for allowing me to play Disney soundtracks for many, many, many hours on end in our apartment while I wrote this book.

Olivia and Lizz for being my people when others around us were telling us we were told old for Disney.

Most importantly, I want to thank Walt Disney. The most incredible part of The Walt Disney Company was that this all started with one man's dream—a dream that we all get to experience to this day. To have your dream become a reality is one thing, but to have it grow in such a way that it's still being enjoyed around the world today is pure magic.

Bounders

Abigail C., as Alice, p. 34
Abigail G., as WALL•E, p. 144
Aki A., as Mary Poppins, p. 139
Alex R., as R2-D2, p. 135
Alexxus C., as the Mad Hatter, p. 102
Alice H., as Rapunzel, p. 92
Alisa W., as Baymax, p. 108
Allison E., as Disgust, p. 155
Alyssa A., as Bo Peep, p. 145
Alyssa S., as Elsa, p. 145
Amber A., as Dumbo, p. 2
Anna B., as Darth Vader, p. 135
Anne G., as Sebastian, p. 137
April F., as Mr. Pricklepants, p. 136
April P., as EVE, p. 144; as Cinderella, p. 147
April U., as Remy, p. 94
Ashley W., as Captain Marvel, p. xviii
Audrey Y., as Goofy, p. 143
Autumn S., as BB-8, p. 135
Baraciel A., as José Carioca, p. 50
Beatriz S., as Boo, p. 3
Bethany R., as Snow White, p. 92
Briana R., as Pluto, p. 143
Brittani E., as Thumper, p. 44
Bryan M., as Hercules, p. 143
Brynne G., as Thor, p. 65
Cailey L., as Addison, p. 134
Caleigh A., Mickey Mouse, p. 48
Cameron K., as José Carioca, p. 50
Camilla K., as Anna, p. 90
Carol S., as Captain Hook, p. 88
Carlanda W., as Scar, p. 56
Charles M., as Carl Fredricksen, p. 82
Charlotte B., as Winnie the Pooh, p. 42
Chelsea H., as Minnie, p. 144
Chip P., as Aladdin, p. 73
Christina M., as Mickey Mouse, p. 143
Christina S., as Ariel, p. 142
Colette V., as Donald Duck, p. 143
Colton T., as Sally, p. 62
Courtney Q., as Pinocchio, p. 60
Danielle G., as Lilo, p. 72
Debbie V., as *Star Wars*, p. 113
Destiny W., as Goofy, p. 18
Dolly G., as Jane, p. 87
Dominique B., as Daisy Duck, p. 138
Erica C., as Mulan as Ping, p. 54
Erika K., as Anna, p. 145
Evonne L., as Jasmine, p. 73
Francis D., as Mickey Mouse, p. 74
Gabe G., as Stitch, p. 72
Genesis C., as Alice, p. 102
Gloria B., as Snow White, p. 130

Gwenan W., as Lilo, p. 100
Heather T., as Rapunzel, p. 139
Ilana G., as Andy's Room, p. 114
Jade A., as Winnie the Pooh, p. 72
Jane C., as Stitch, p. 56
James H., as Megara, p. 135
Janelly A., as Lightning McQueen, p. 80
Jasem A., as Aladdin, p. 58
Jennifer B., as Rapunzel, p. 142
Jennifer G., as Indiana Jones, p. 87
Jennifer S., as Grumpy, p. 46
Jeremy R., as Woody, p. 98
Jessica M., as Minnie Mouse, p. 143
Jessica M., as Tiana, p. 92
Jessica W., as Aurora, p. 92
Joanna G., as pineapple soft serve, p. 118
Julia S., as Mr. Smee, p. 38
June J., as Rapunzel, p. 40
Kana N., as Cinderella, p. 135
Karamia L., as WALL•E, p. 158
Karen P., as Marie, p. 136
Kate M., as Ursula, p. 68
Katherine L., as Moana, p. 76
Katsie L., as Ariel, p. 104
Katsuhisa A., as Bert, p. 139
Keshia S., as Mulan, p. 136
Kelly J., as Merida, p. 36
Kelly V., as Megara, p. 143
Kelsey W., as Rex, p. 136
Kirk S., as Aladdin, p. 158
Kirsten L., as the Blue Fairy, p. 145
Kirstie L., as the Haunted Mansion Ride Attendant, p. 124
Kristen K., as Elsa, p. 66
Lauren G., as Donald Duck, p. 14
Leo C., as Mickey Mouse, p. 10
Leslie K., as Dr. Facilier, p. x; as a Lost Boy twin, p. xiii; as Winnie the Pooh, p. xiv; as Minnie Mouse, p. 12; and as the Incredible Hulk, p. 127
Lindsay B., as R2-D2, p. 132
Lizzy J., as Hercules, p. 135
Lyssa C., as Moana, p. 73
Madison W., as Darth Vader, p. 132
Malerie M., as Judy Hopps, p. 139
Maria L., as Ursula, p. 104
Maryssa L., as Winnie the Pooh, p. 144
Mascha D., as Daisy Duck, p. 16
Megan D., as Hades, p. 140
Monica F., as the Haunted Mansion Tightrope Walker, p. 122

Natazsa R., as Buzz Lightyear, p. 30
Nicole K., as Belle, p. 69
Nicole M., as Jasmine, p. 128
Paola P., as Tiana, p. 28
Patrick D., as the Magic Carpet, p. 73
Pernell L., as Doctor Strange, p. 142
Rachel B., as Gaston, p. 137
Ranitra C., as Flower, p. 143
Rayna L., as Tadashi Hamada, p. 108
Samantha O., as Cinderella, p. 150
Sara C., as Mulan, p. 52
Sarah G., as Anastasia Tremaine, p. 20
Sarah R., as Rey, p. 135
Shannon A., as the Hyena, p. 56
Stephanie G., as Buzz Lightyear, p. 138
Sumer L., as C-3PO, p. 132
Sydney L., as Hiro Hamada, p. 108
Tanya M., as Ellie Fredricksen, p. 82
Taylor Y., as the Indiana Jones Adventure ride, p. 117
Teresa M., as Figment, p. 84
Tessa W., as Rapunzel, p. 96
Tiffany M., as Drizella Tremaine, p. 20
Tiffany R., as Ariel, p. 158
Tiffany S., as Daisy Duck, p. 143
Tisha K., as Ursula, p. 22
Traci H., as Ariel, p. 26
Tristin C., as Mickey Mouse, p. 57
Tyler H., as Zed, p. 134
Tyler S., as Jack, p. 62
Utako Y., as Vanellope von Schweetz, p. 70
Vanessa H., as the Haunted Mansion ride, p. 120
William B., as Mr. Toad, p. 78
Yasmine O., as Rapunzel, p. 158
Yvette A., as Buttercup, p. 136
Zhengyi A., as Duffy, p. 106

Index

accessories, xiii, 3, 4, 5, 6, 7, 8, 11, 13, 15, 16, 17, 23, 24, 25, 27, 31, 32, 33, 34, 36, 38, 39, 40, 41, 42, 43, 44, 45, 46, 47, 51, 58, 59, 64, 65, 67, 68, 69, 88, 89, 91, 94, 95, 98, 99, 103, 106, 107, 110, 112, 114, 115, 116, 118, 119, 120, 121, 126, 127, 129, 135, 137, 142, 144, 145
Addison (*Z-O-M-B-I-E-S*), 134
Adventures by Disney, 87, 90
Aladdin, 4, 58, 59, 73, 105, 158
Aladdin, 4, 7, 24, 32, 51, 58, 59, 73, 105, 111, 128, 129, 158
Alice, 34, 35, 69, 93, 102
Alice in Wonderland, 34, 35, 93, 101, 102, 103
Aliens (Toy Story), 7, 114, 115
Andy's Room, 114
Anna, 87, 90, 91 130, 145
aprons, 34, 69
Ariel, 26, 27, 28, 72, 104, 142, 148, 158
Aristocats, The, 111, 136
Aulani, 73, 75, 76, 77, 106
Aurora, 5, 92
backstage, xvi
bags, 5, 7, 8, 11, 13, 24, 25, 27, 28, 29, 35, 37, 41, 42, 43, 44, 45, 51, 58, 59, 107, 119, 120, 123, 129, 137, 152
Bambi, 44, 45, 143
Baymax, 108
BB-8, 135
Beauty and the Beast, 6, 7, 69, 111, 112, 135, 137
Belle, 6, 7, 69, 111, 112
Bert (*Mary Poppins*), 139
Big Hero 6, 108
Blue Fairy, 145
Bo Peep, 114, 145
Boo, 3
Bounds, Lillian, xiii
bows (hair), 12, 13, 15, 16, 17, 32, 33 34, 35, 130, 138
Brave, 6, 36, 37, 51, 68, 87
brown boots, 6, 7, 19, 36, 47, 98, 99, 115, 152
Bullseye (Toy Story), 115

Buttercup (*Toy Story 3*), 136
Buzz Lightyear, 5, 30, 31, 115, 138
C-3PO, 132
capes, 65, 66, 91, 153
Captain Hook, 39, 86, 88, 89
Captain Marvel, xviii
Carl Fredricksen, 82
Cars, 79, 80, 81
cast member, xvi, 88, 116, 124, 135
Chewbacca, 6
Cinderella, 20, 24, 51, 68, 135, 142, 147, 150
Cinderella, 24, 51, 68, 135, 146, 147, 150
Claw (Toy Story), 115
color blocking, 3, 4, 5, 7, 10, 26, 30, 34, 42, 52, 90, 102, 106, 107, 110, 127, 130
colored pants, 7, 9, 10, 11, 26, 51, 152
Constance Hatchaway, 121, 122
CookieAnn, 105
Cruella De Vil, 4, 51, 148
Daisy Duck, 6, 9, 16, 17, 32, 75, 138, 143
Dapper Days, viii, 138
Darth Vader, 132, 135
Disgust (*Inside Out*), 155
Disney California Adventure, 79, 81
Disney Cruise Line, 86, 88
Disneyland, viii, 72, 79, 127, 137, 143
Disneyland Paris, 72, 93, 94, 95
Disney's Port Orleans Resort—Riverside, xiii
Disney Villains, 51, 111
Disney, Walt, xiii, 10, 79, 154
Doctor Strange, 143
Dole Whip, 116, 118, 119
Donald Duck, 6, 9, 14, 15, 16, 17, 75, 143
Dory, 7
Dr. Facilier, x
Duffy the Disney Bear, 75, 105, 106, 107
Dumbo, 2
DVC (Disney Vacation Club), xvii
Edna Mode, 65
Ellie Fredricksen, 82

Elsa, 7, 65, 66, 67, 91, 145
Emperor's New Groove, The, 51
Epcot, 65, 83
EVE, 144
Extra Magic Hours, xvii
FastPass+, xvii
Figment, 83, 84, 85, 116
Finding Nemo, 7
Fix-It Felix, 51
Flit, 57, 97
Flounder, 7, 27
Flower (*Bambi*), 143
Frozen, 7, 65, 66, 67, 90, 91, 145
Gaston, 69, 137
Gelatoni, 105
Genie, 4, 7, 32, 51, 105, 111, 149
glasses, 15, 17, 32, 34, 35, 39, 59, 85
Goofy, 6, 9, 18, 19, 75, 143
Grumpy, 46, 47
Guardians of the Galaxy, 111
guest, xvi, xvii, 3, 65, 68, 79, 124, 125, 153
Hades, 140
hair accessories, 12, 13, 15, 16, 17, 27, 29, 33, 34, 35, 37, 38, 41, 55, 68, 119, 125, 129, 130, 138
Han Solo, 64
hats, 7, 11, 14, 18, 19, 27, 31, 38, 43, 46, 47, 58, 59, 68, 89, 95, 99, 102, 103, 106
Haunted Mansion, the, 97, 120, 121, 122, 123, 124, 125
Hercules, 87, 135, 143
Hercules, xv, 87, 135, 140, 143
Hidden Mickeys, xvii
Hiro Hamada, 108
Hong Kong Disneyland, 65, 72, 73, 97, 98, 99, 106
Hyena, 56
Incredible Hulk, 127
Incredibles, The, 65
Inside Out, 155
Jack Skellington, 8, 62
Jasmine, 7, 24, 51, 73, 126, 128, 129
Jessie, 115

Art by Anum Tariq

Designed by Lindsay Broderick

Editorial by Erin Zimring

Library of Congress Control Number: 2019957143
ISBN 978-1-368-05042-5
FAC-038091-20059
Printed in the United States of America
First Paperback Edition, April 2020
1 3 5 7 9 10 8 6 4 2
Visit www.disneybooks.com

D23
The Official Disney Fan Club
D23.com

jewelry, 5, 8, 9, 13, 24, 25, 29, 32, 35, 37, 39, 41, 42, 43, 45, 47, 51, 53, 55, 58, 64, 65, 67, 77, 81, 85, 89, 91, 95, 99, 119, 121, 123, 125, 129
José Carioca, 50
Journey Into Imagination, 83, 84, 85, 116
Judy Hopps, 139
key pieces, 6
King Triton, 46
kitschy bags, 7, 25, 35, 37, 119
Lightning McQueen, 79, 80, 81
Lilo, 72, 75, 100, 137, 138
Lilo & Stitch, 7, 51, 56, 72, 75, 100, 137
Lion King, The, 6, 7, 56
Little Mermaid, The, 7, 22, 26, 27, 28, 46, 51, 72, 104, 126, 137, 142, 148, 158
Mad Hatter, 101, 102, 103
Madame Leota, 121
MagicBand, xvii
Magic Carpet, the, 58, 73, 111
Magical Express, xvi
Maleficent, 51
Marvel, 127
Mary Poppins, 139
Mary Poppins, 139
Meeko, 57, 97
Megara, 135, 143
Memory Maker, xvii
Merida, 6, 36, 37, 51, 68, 87
Merlin, 46
Michael Darling, 8, 97
Mickey Mouse, xvii, 6, 9, 10, 11, 12, 48, 51, 74, 75, 105, 116, 143
Minnie Mouse, 6, 9, 12, 13, 17, 75, 105, 136, 138, 143, 144, 148
Moana, 73, 75, 76, 77, 148
Moana, 73, 75, 76, 77, 148
Monsters, Inc., 3
Mother Gothel, 65
Mr. Pricklepants, 136
Mr. Smee, 38, 39
Mr. Toad, 78
Mulan, 24, 32, 52, 53, 54, 55, 64, 68, 70, 136, 149
Mulan, 24, 32, 52, 53, 54, 55, 64, 68, 70, 136, 149
Mushu, 53

Nightmare Before Christmas, The, 8, 62
'Olu Mel, 105
One Hundred and One Dalmatians, 4, 51, 156
Peter Pan, 9, 51, 93, 97
Peter Pan, 8, 9, 38, 39, 51, 88, 89, 93, 97
pineapple soft serve, 116, 118, 119
Ping (Mulan), 54, 55
Pinocchio, 60, 145
pins, 25, 31, 114, 115
pirates, 38, 39, 86, 88, 93, 101, 116
Pirate Night, 86, 88
Pluto, 7, 143
Pocahontas, 57, 97
Prince Charming, 51
Prince Eric, 126
Prince Phillip, 25
Princess and the Frog, The, x, 28, 29, 69, 92, 126, 149
Princess Leia, 24
prom, 3, 126, 128, 129
props, 2, 3, 5, 8, 35, 55, 64, 153
Queen, the (Snow White and the Seven Dwarfs), 65
R2-D2, 113, 132, 135
Rajah, 24, 129
Rapunzel, xiii, xiv, 24, 40, 41, 92, 139, 142, 146, 158
Ratatouille, 60, 93, 94, 95
Remy, 93, 94, 95
Redd (Pirates of the Caribbean), 116
Rex, 114, 115, 136
Rey, 135
Robin Hood, 5, 8
Rocket Raccoon, 111
rope drop, xvii
RunDisney, 127
Sally, 62
Scar, 56
scarves, 33, 44, 45, 46, 47, 106
Sebastian, 27, 137
Seven Dwarfs, 46, 47
Shanghai Disneyland, 72, 101, 106
ShellieMay, 75, 105
Sherman, Robert B., ix
silhouette, 5, 9, 11, 15, 16, 17, 26, 30, 51, 53, 57, 106, 112, 122, 123, 128

Simba, 6, 7
Sleeping Beauty, 5, 25, 51, 92
Snow White, 5, 6, 92, 111, 127, 130, 131, 148
Snow White and the Seven Dwarfs, 5, 6, 46, 47, 65, 92, 111, 127, 130, 131, 148
solid-color tees, 7
Star Wars, 6, 24, 64, 113, 132, 135
StellaLou, 105
Stitch, 7, 51, 56, 72, 75, 137, 138
Sword in the Stone, The, 46
Tadashi Hamada, 108
Tangled, xiii, xiv, 24, 40, 41, 65, 92, 139, 142, 146, 158
Thor, 8, 64, 65
Thumper, 44, 45
Tiana, 28, 29, 69, 92, 126, 149
Tightrope Walker (The Haunted Mansion), 122, 123
Tokyo Disneyland, 72, 105, 106, 107
Tokyo DisneySea, 105
Toy Story, 5, 6, 7, 30, 31, 97, 98, 99, 114, 115, 136, 138, 145
Tremaine sisters, 20
Trixie, 136
Up, 82
Ursula, 22, 51, 104
Vanellope von Schweetz, 126
vibe, 5, 6, 17, 21, 39, 40, 44, 52, 55, 59, 68, 76, 89, 98, 99, 106, 116, 118, 122, 124, 128
vintage, 14, 64, 102, 103, 120, 134, 139, 145
WALL•E, 144, 158
WALL•E, 144, 158
Walt Disney World, xii, xiii, xvi, xvii, 65, 72, 83, 84, 86, 127
weapons, 5, 8, 25, 37, 64, 121
wigs, 3, 33, 68
Winnie the Pooh, xiv, 24, 42, 43, 72, 144
Woody, 6, 97, 98, 99, 114
Wreck-It Ralph, 51
yellow shoes, 6, 9, 10, 11, 12, 14, 15, 29, 42, 43, 118, 119, 144, 152
Yzma, 51
Zed (Z-O-M-B-I-E-S), 134
Z-O-M-B-I-E-S, 134
Zootopia, 139